UniK PSYCHO-SALES MODEL™

A MODEL IN WHICH THE INTEGRATED ADULT EGO STATE SUPPORTS COGNITIVE SELLING

DR. UNNIKRISHNAN T.T

INDIA · SINGAPORE · MALAYSIA

Dedicated to the Divine Force

For

Guiding My Thoughts, Feelings, and Behaviour.

Contents

The Person Behind This Book

Dr. Unnikrishnan, creator of the UniK Psycho-Sales Model, is a professional with experience in management, education, and mentorship. Three decades of experience selling office furniture in Bahrain have furthered his marketing and communication skills, as well as his understanding of market trends. Additionally, he has been actively involved in imparting knowledge and conducting sessions for accredited courses, thereby fostering learning and professional development. He orchestrates the Youth Leadership Program for students, emphasising leadership development and mentorship.

Recognition for excellence - Received the Award for Excellence in Mentoring from the Asia Education Conclave, Bangkok, Thailand. The Best Faculty Award, the Best Mentor Award, and the Platinum Award for Group Counselling from PGF Bahrain. A public speaker, Dr. Unnikrishnan held esteemed positions, including President of Toastmasters Clubs, Area 5 Director, and Vice-President of the PGF Counselling Research Club. He is involved in raising awareness about various psychological topics through public lectures and is a member of the Kerala Clinical Counsellors Association (KCCA).

Acknowledgements

This book on the "UniK Psycho-Sales Model" has its roots in my extensive research for my Doctoral Program. When I reflect on this journey, I am reminded of the following words of Alfred North Whitehead:

> "No one who achieves success does so without acknowledging the help of others.

> The wise and confident acknowledge this help with gratitude."

> – Alfred North Whitehead

At the outset, I would like to express my gratitude to my mentor, Dr. John Panackel, a Counselling Psychologist, for planting the seeds of wisdom in me. I want to thank Dr. Sanjib Chakraborty, Founder and President of East Bridge University in Paris, for his guidance and support. I sincerely appreciate the fantastic support of European International University and East Bridge University faculty members throughout this journey.

I am grateful to my wife, Distinguished Toastmaster Kamala Unnikrishnan; my son, Rajith Unnikrishnan; and my daughter, Ramya Unnikrishnan, for their unwavering cooperation and encouragement.

I thank my colleagues, Mr. Khushroo Mowdawala (General Manager), Mr. Sandeep Reynold (Showroom In-charge), Mr. Janeesh Raj (Designer), Ms. Diana Pinto (Administration),

Mr. Govind Naik (Stores In-charge), Mr. Alwyn Noronha (Sales Executive), and Ms. Karen Acebedo Mamba (Sales Executive), for their cooperation and support throughout this journey.

I am thankful to all those who participated in my survey and expert interviews for their valuable feedback and suggestions.

I am grateful to the members of the Toastmasters fraternity and the Pravasi Guidance Forum for their support and motivation.

I appreciate my late parents' efforts in instilling a growth mindset in me and fostering my personal and professional development.

Finally, I would like to thank the readers for their encouragement and support.

Dr. Unnikrishnan T.T.

Author's Note

Welcome to the UniK Psycho-Sales Model (the word "UniK" is derived from my name). I appreciate your interest in exploring this sales model in which the Integrated Adult ego state supports Cognitive selling.

The idea for this book came to me after my dissertation defence for my Doctoral Programme at the European International University, where I presented the UniK Psycho-Sales Model – a result of my extensive research and literature review on the topic "Identifying the Role of the Integrated Adult Ego State in the Cognitive Selling Approach: A Study on Office Furniture in the Kingdom of Bahrain." The Dissertation Committee suggested making this resource available to the sales fraternity. Later, when I presented this model, the PGF Counsellors Research Club, Toastmasters Clubs, and Dr. John Panackel suggested that I write a book on the topic to make it accessible to everyone.

This book is divided into an Introduction, Theory, Research Work, and the UniK Psycho-Sales Model. Selling is a practice employed in all walks of life. Everybody sells to get things done. As you turn the pages, you will realise that this is useful to Business Professionals, Sales Professionals, Customers, Educators, Trainers, and the General Public.

This book is organised to be read sequentially, allowing you to apply theory to practice. While writing this book,

I utilised AI to provide layers of information, facilitating a deeper understanding of the concept. Although I have attempted to cite all sources and contributions, some specific ideas or sentences may have inadvertently emerged from my memory due to the influence of past experiences. Any omissions in citations are entirely unintentional. Please notify me of any citations that lack proper acknowledgement, so that I can take corrective action.

This model creates self-awareness and strengthens salespeople's ability to achieve success. I have successfully implemented this model in sales.

I invite you to understand this model, apply it in practice, and achieve success in sales.

Wishing you an enriching experience.

Sincerely,

Dr. Unnikrishnan T.T.

Foreword

Selling is based on human interactions—direct or indirect, depending on the products sold. Hence, it becomes imperative to understand Human Psychology. The UniK Psycho-Sales Model, developed by Dr. Unnikrishnan during his Doctoral Research program, is based on Transactional Analysis and Cognitive Selling sales approaches. Transactional Analysis (TA) is a transformative theory of personality and psychotherapy that improves human interactions, communication patterns, and emotional dynamics. This model demonstrates that Transactional Analysis facilitates cognitive selling by understanding the psychology of customers, enabling sales to be customer-focused and address their specific needs and motivations.

This diagrammatically represented model explains the various stages of sales interactions with examples from his experience. This helps the reader understand how the salesperson and customer think, feel, and behave during their interactions. This book covers the relevant aspects of Transactional Analysis, Cognitive Selling Sales Approach, Cognitive Biases, and Research Findings for comprehensive reading.

The chapters covered under Part IV, UniK Psycho-Sales Model, help the reader walk through the model and experience the entire sales process in real time. This model explains the thought process and behavioural aspects of both the salesperson and the customer, the challenges the salesperson faces, the impact of cognitive biases in sales, and the methods adopted to overcome these obstacles. This helps the reader understand the tips and tricks of selling.

Since the model focuses on the Integrated Adult ego state, for the benefit of readers, the book provides guidelines on adopting this ego state. This developed or matured ego state facilitates effective decision-making, balanced communication, conflict resolution, and the development of a growth mindset. It also explains the inputs required for creating an Integrated Adult ego state and the outcomes that result from it. The outcomes justifiably support Cognitive selling. This model aims to psychologically strengthen salespeople, create value, deliver exceptional customer service, and foster stronger customer bonds, ultimately leading to repeat purchases.

I recommend this book to enthusiastic readers with great pleasure. It will enrich their psychodynamic skills and empower them in their careers.

Dr. John Panackel

Counselling Psychologist

International Life Coach.

PART I:

INTRODUCTION

Chapter 1

Jubilant Journey

"Success is stumbling from failure to failure with no loss of enthusiasm."

– Winston S. Churchill

People say success comes from failures. This paradoxical statement metaphorically conveys that failures act as stepping stones for success. This can be achieved only when we learn from failures and apply those learnings in appropriate situations; otherwise, failure remains a failure, making it difficult to overcome. Learning from failures is a continuous process leading to growth and development.

In the initial stages of my sales career, a sequence of failures enveloped me. This was disappointing and frustrating. Experiencing failure made me uncertain about my future as I began to internalise it. However, my passion for sales made me resilient and perseverant. I did not want to leave my sales career. I asked myself how to turn all my failures into opportunities for growth. This made me think. I realised that, although a college education provided a strong foundation for a sales career, other skills were also required for sales success. Formal sales training from experienced professionals, personality traits, and the ability to adapt to different clients, markets, and situations could contribute to sales success. I started working on myself and equipped myself with the skills and knowledge for success in sales. Later, I could work in professionally managed companies as a sales manager. I moved from my Motherland to the Middle East. Here, I learned counselling, which transformed me and equipped me with the tools to help people navigate their challenges. While learning counselling, I became passionate about specialising in Transactional Analysis (TA). The skills and knowledge I acquired from TA had a significant impact on both my professional and personal life.

In 2020, COVID-19 had a profoundly negative impact on the entire world. I could experience and explore the perils and pains of being a salesperson. Salespeople were unable to leave the office to meet customers. The market was not responsive. Demand for products declined. Salespeople's morale came down. Under such circumstances, I realised that one should understand the psychological impact on salespeople. How can we strengthen the salespersons and prevent emotional breakdowns? At the same time, I learned how to understand customers from the proper perspective. By examining Eric Berne's Transactional Analysis Theory and the Cognitive Selling sales approach, I discovered solutions to these critical issues in my research. My research culminated in the creation of the UniK Psycho-Sales Model, where the Integrated Adult ego state supports Cognitive Selling. This model uses the Integrated Adult ego state of the salesperson to understand customer needs and preferences psychologically.

In short, the UniK Psycho-Sales Model serves as a bridge between theory and practice, yielding improved sales performance and client satisfaction, and making a meaningful contribution to the sales field.

The Journey Continues... Read On...

Chapter 2

Meaning-Full is Meaningful

"Communication is only effective when we communicate in a way that is meaningful to the recipient, not ourselves."

– Rich Simmonds

In 2024, my family and I visited Bangkok. When we touched down at Suvarnabhumi Airport, the cordiality and helpful nature of the Thai people made us feel at home. They guided me to take a taxi to the pre-booked hotel. The taxi driver greeted us and was more than happy to help us with our luggage. He was friendly and easy to deal with. However, I faced a linguistic barrier while conversing as he was not proficient in English. Very often, he struggled with grammar and vocabulary while talking.

I wanted to engage in a meaningful conversation to learn about the places. However, the responses I received were indifferent and lacked genuine enthusiasm. He was kind enough to bridge the gap and steer the conversation meaningfully using Google Translate and his body language. This experience has enlightened me about the significance of clear communication in conversations and understanding the meaning of what others are saying.

Today, we live in an interconnected and dynamic world that requires clear communication. Our messages can be purposeful only when understood in the intended way.

Proper use of vocabulary, technology, non-verbal skills, or acquiring new languages can achieve this, which is conducive to fostering better relationships and understanding among people from diverse backgrounds.

When a message is full of meaning or rich with layers of meaning, it becomes a meaningful form of communication. Meaningful communication plays a crucial role in both our personal and professional lives. Now, the question arises: How do we make communication meaningful? To communicate meaningfully is a skill that can be learned. To master this particular skill, we must first learn to communicate effectively with ourselves and then with others. We should be able to analyse and understand how our interactions and behaviours affect others in the communication process. While communicating, it is not what we say that is important, but what meaning the other person assigns to what we say determines the outcome of the communication. Communication becomes complex when verbal and non-verbal elements, emotions, and personal biases are intertwined.

The meaning of our communication depends upon the following:

a. The vocabulary: Words are instrumental in informing, instructing, influencing, and inspiring people. They enhance clarity and can evoke emotions in others. The appropriate words and expressions convey the message and emotions meaningfully.

b. Paralinguistic factors: Non-verbal cues such as pitch, volume, and modulation of a spoken language constitute paralinguistic factors. They are independent of the words used and can change the meaning of the spoken message.

c. Body language: These are non-verbal cues expressed through facial expressions, eye movements, postures, gestures, and movements. It conveys emotions, attitudes, and intentions behind the spoken words. While communicating, most of the body language happens without our conscious awareness. Body language comes from our subconscious mind. When we speak, people typically observe our bodies first - our faces, eyes, gestures, postures, attire, and so on - and conclude. This means our body speaks to them first. We convey our inner thoughts, feelings, and attitudes through body language. This happens as our brain tends to prioritise non-verbal communication over verbal communication.

d. Context: The setting under which communication occurs is known as the context. Relationships, time, and situational factors influence the message. The context or situation assigns meaning to what we say. For example, consider a simple message: 'What is the time now?' Depending on the situation, this question can have different implications:

- When asked casually, it simply means the person wants to know the current time.

- If an employee enters the office late, the boss might ask, 'What is the time?' In this case, it implies that the employee is late and is not allowed.

- When a boy watches a late-night movie at home, his mother might ask, 'What time is it?' Here, it implies that it is time for him to go to bed.

In summary, the meanings change with context.

Similarly, people in healthy relationships habitually use language with meanings originating from their shared experiences that outsiders may not understand.

We have to understand the dynamics of communication to make it meaningful. Meaningful communication facilitates the sharing of information, fosters connections, helps individuals comprehend emotions, and cultivates more profound relationships. It builds strong relationships and fosters growth. Thus, meaningful communication is conducive to personal and professional development.

Keep Reading... There is More to Know...

Chapter 3

The Person in the Salesperson

"Great Salespeople are relationship builders who provide value and help their customers win,"

– Jeffrey Gitomer

Having held a sales job, I fully concur with the above statement. I have noticed that a strong rapport with customers is crucial to a salesperson's success. They win the trust and confidence of the customers by understanding their requirements and finding solutions to their challenges. Salespeople are problem solvers who offer acceptable solutions to customers, benefiting both parties. A good relationship leads to retention, so that when a customer needs to be serviced again, they are more likely to return to the salesperson. This ensures long-term loyalty. Loyalty is a crucial factor in sales, as it generates repeat purchases at a minimal cost. A loyal customer base will give a competitive advantage over other companies. Thus, loyalty not only strengthens customer relationships but also boosts profits.

Through the phrase 'person in the salesperson,' I aim to emphasise the significance of the individual's identity, thought process, and behavioural patterns beyond the realm of professional jargon. The person is the centre point. Customers view the salesperson as a reflection of the company they serve. Their behaviour, knowledge, personality, and professionalism reflect the company's image. This person plays a pivotal role in generating revenue for the organisation and ensuring business viability. They safeguard their interest by prioritising the customer's interests. He can influence the purchasing decisions. They serve as a vital link between the company and its customers. The customers also evaluate the salesperson before making a purchasing decision. The qualities of a salesperson are crucial in winning the hearts of customers. I have noticed that customers tend to buy from the salesman with whom they are most comfortable. He can retain customers to the company's benefit. Hence, a salesperson plays a pivotal role in the success and growth of businesses. A competent salesperson is an asset to the organisation.

I observed that qualities such as active listening, empathy, confidence, enthusiasm, resilience, organisation, and honesty contribute to a salesperson's success. However, a salesperson becomes exceptional when these traits are combined with product knowledge and strong interpersonal skills. The success of salespeople can be equated with the success of companies.

Curious to Strengthen?... Keep Reading...

Chapter 4

Strengthening Salespersons

"Sales are contingent upon the attitude of the salesman, not the attitude of the prospect."

– William Clement Stone

In a competitive market, salespeople play a pivotal role. I view them as "ambassadors of business houses" as they bridge the connection between businesses and customers. They contribute to revenue through sales and maintain better customer relations. They collect relevant information about the market, customer choices, competition, and changing scenarios, which helps in strategy formation.

Fierce competition generally leads to a 'price war.' Competitors slash prices. With this strategy, I have seen many businesses ultimately lose the war, as profits dwindle. This ultimately led to the closure of their operations. One way to generate healthy revenues is by strengthening the salesforce. Make them more competitive. Invest in their skill development. They can create better experiences through tailor-made solutions, friendliness, and building confidence in customers. Most customers are willing to pay more for an experience with a confident and convincing salesperson.

In a competitive market, salespeople face challenges that make selling difficult. Rejections from customers lead to demotivation. Sometimes, prospects may become challenging to handle and waste time. Thus, a sales job becomes a battle difficult to win. Result: stress levels increase, confidence levels deteriorate, and personal life and relationships suffer. We should remember that every salesperson is a human with heart and soul. He or she is an emotional being controlled by their thoughts. Thoughts play a vital role in creating feelings, behaviour, and mindset. Hence, a salesperson needs to be strengthened at the cognitive level.

I have utilised Transactional Analysis (TA) and the Cognitive Selling approach to help salespeople overcome challenges and achieve success. TA is a psychoanalytical theory and psychotherapy created by Dr Eric Berne, a Canadian psychiatrist and psychoanalyst, during the 1950s. Transactional Analysis (TA) equips us to enhance communication and self-awareness, and develop stronger customer rapport. The cognitive selling sales approach helps to comprehend the mindset and behaviour patterns of the customers. This comprehension enables the creation of customer-focused interactions, ultimately leading to a successful sales outcome that benefits both parties.

Ready for the Next Part?... Let us Move Ahead...

P A R T II:

A DIVE INTO THEORY

Chapter 5

Preparing the Ground

"To truly understand the complex, we must first master
the basics."

– Alfred North Whitehead

Understanding the basics is essential to comprehending any complex subject. This will help us overcome the subject's complexities. Once thoroughly familiar with the basics, it provides a strong foundation for solving complex problems. Understanding the fundamental concepts helps us grasp the intricacies of the subject, thereby improving our cognitive abilities.

In the UniK Psycho-Sales Model, I have incorporated the principles of Transactional Analysis (TA) and Cognitive Selling. Both of these subjects have psychological aspects. TA is defined as a theory of personality and psychotherapy. Cognitive selling combines psychology with a strategic approach to sales effectiveness. These two subjects are fascinating as they provide valuable insights into analysing and understanding human behaviour and the secrets of human interactions. Hence, I have covered these subjects in detail. To make the reading more enjoyable, I have incorporated diagrams and figures to facilitate easy understanding.

I hope that readers will comprehend the model, allowing them to grasp its principles and concepts. They should understand the various components of the model to appreciate its purpose and relevance to different market segments. Once this model is understood, implementing it step by step becomes easy. This comprehensive model encompasses a wide range of topics applicable to all face-to-face selling scenarios.

Keep Going... There is More to Fathom...

Chapter 6

Unlocking the TA Treasure Chest

"The destiny of every human being is decided by what goes on inside his skull when confronted by what goes on outside his skull."

– Dr. Eric Berne

Dr. Eric Berne emphasises the significance of our inner thoughts, which shape our destiny. These inner thoughts occur in our brains, whether we are aware of them or not, and generate emotional energies that translate into actions or behaviour. Pleasant or positive thoughts lead to acceptable or productive behaviour, while negative thoughts may result in undesirable outcomes.

It is common to observe varying behaviours when conversing with our prospects or customers. I have seen customers behaving differently at different times. Sometimes, they become expressive, playful, or even obedient. Other times, they become judgemental, authoritative, caring, and supportive. They even become rational, logical, open-minded, and open to new information. Why do customers interact in these ways? The answer we get from Transactional Analysis unlocks the secrets of communication, relationships, and personal growth.

6.1 Transactional Analysis (TA):

TA is a psychoanalytical theory and therapy created by Dr. Eric Berne, a Canadian psychiatrist and psychoanalyst, during the 1950s. He developed the concept and paradigm of TA to explain human behaviour (*Transactional Analysis (TA): Overview, Examples, and Effectiveness*, 2023). The International Transactional Analysis Association suggests that "Transactional Analysis is a theory of personality and a systematic psychotherapy for personal growth and change" (Stewart & Joines, 1987).

Transactional Analysis is concerned with the following analysis:

1. Ego state analysis to analyse the communication exchanges between people. It consists of

    i. Structural Analysis to analyse the individual personality and

    ii. Functional Analysis to analyse the observed behaviour of a person.

2. Transactional Analysis (proper) to analyse how people interact with one another.

3. Game Analysis to analyse ulterior transactions leading to a payoff.

4. Script Analysis helps individuals become aware of unconsciously made early decisions about how to live, understand the reasons for such decisions, and learn how to stop making such limiting patterns of decisions.

5. Stroke Analysis to study the exchange of strokes between individuals (James & Jongeward, 1981).

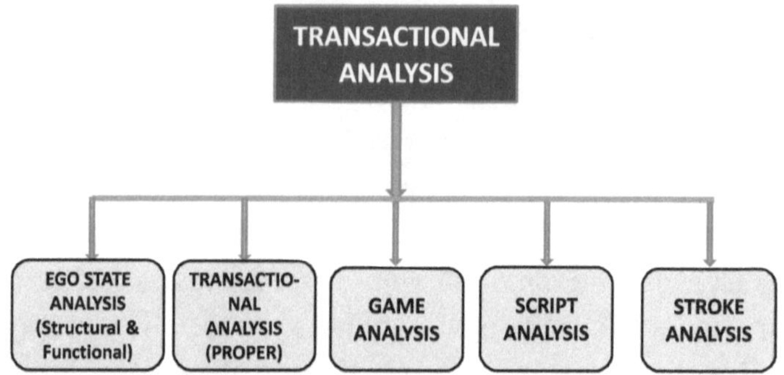

Figure 1: Analysis under Transactional Analysis. Recreated by Unnikrishnan T.T. based on (*Born to Win: Transactional Analysis with Gestalt Experiments*, n.d.)

6.2 Benefits of TA:

Transactional Analysis is a powerful tool for personal growth and change with the following benefits: (Stewart & Joines, 1987)

1. It enhances communication and fosters productive interactions between individuals. Hence, it benefits anyone interested in improving their communication (Qureshi, 2024)

2. It gives an insight into understanding human behaviour and why people behave as they do. (Sc-Admin, 2024)

3. It fosters self-awareness and enhances critical thinking. It throws light on one's dysfunctional behaviours and communication patterns (Sc-Admin, 2024)

4. Puts an end to repetitive damaging patterns of behaviour. This will help to develop better relationships with people (Qureshi, 2024)

5. Reconciles Conflicts, confusion, and tensions with relationships (Weil, 2023)

6. Enhances harmonious work environments and fosters better relationships in organisations, leading to higher productivity (Weil, 2023)

7. It is a psychotherapy for treating psychological disorders (Stewart & Joines, 1987)

6.3 Philosophy of TA:

The philosophy of TA is based on three assumptions (Stewart & Joines, 1987). These are as follows:

- *People are OK*: This means everyone has worth, value, and dignity as people. People are acceptable as they are, but may not accept or like what they do. This is a statement that describes the inherent nature of a person rather than their behaviour. People are all at the same level. This is true even though people may have different accomplishments, geographical locations, races, ages, and religions.

- *Everyone has the capacity to think.* Everyone, except the severely brain-damaged, is capable of thinking. Therefore, all are responsible for deciding what they want from their life. Everyone will ultimately live with the consequences of their decisions.

- *People decide their destinies, and these decisions can be changed.* Any decision one makes can be changed at a later time. One can track these decisions and replace them with new, more appropriate ones if some of these infantile choices lead to unsettling outcomes for them as adults. People can, therefore, change. One brings about change by actively choosing to alter one's previous behavioural patterns, rather than simply becoming aware of them. One can make improvements that stick around.

6.4 Goals of TA:

The goal of Transactional Analysis is:

- To help individuals make new decisions about their current behaviour and change the direction of their lives.

- To increase personal autonomy to enable optimum psychological health and growth.

Thus, the goals of TA are to help individuals gain autonomy, which develops the capacity for awareness, spontaneity, and the ability to form intimate connections with people. This empowers individuals to rectify their unhealthy patterns of life, facilitate personal growth, and shape an individual's destiny (TRANSACTIONAL ANALYSIS by Gerald Corey—*Google Search*, n.d.).

TA blends a practical approach focused on the potential for growth and development with a highly understandable theory for developing people and systems. The personality model used in TA is based on ego states (Cornell & Thunnissen, 2015).

6.5 Ego States Analysis:

In Transactional Analysis (TA), ego states analysis is a technique for analysing the transaction process in interpersonal communication.

The ego state model serves as the cornerstone of Transactional Analysis (TA) theory. An ego state is a state of being that a person experiences at a given time (Stewart & Joines, 1987). Dr. Eric Berne defined ego state as "a consistent pattern of feeling and experience directly related to a corresponding consistent pattern of behavior" (Berne, 2015). An ego state refers to the way one thinks, feels, and behaves at a given moment, thereby shaping one's personality. Although we remain in one ego state, we frequently switch between ego states without realising it. Berne identified three ego states — Parent, Adult, and Child — in which a person's thoughts, feelings, and actions can be categorised (Stewart & Joines, 1987). This conceptualisation closely aligns with the concept of personality. However, the two concepts differ in terms of *transience*. Personality is enduring and internal, but an ego state is fleeting and dependent on the nature of interactions in a particular situation. Ego State is a central concept in Transactional Analysis (TA) (Berne, 2015).

According to TA, the basis of human behaviour is the interaction between three ego states: the Parent, Adult, and Child ego states, collectively referred to as the PAC. These ego states encompass the complete thought, feeling, and behaviour systems one uses to communicate with others. In TA, this basic model of ego states is used in two ways (Cornell & Thunnissen, 2015).

i. Structural analysis reveals a person's personality structure (or the inside), past experiences, and insights responsible for a person's behaviour.

ii. Functional analysis reveals the communicative behaviour of people (the outside), which is observable by others.

6.5.1 The Structural Model of Ego States:

The Theory suggests that our psychological structure (the "inside") is divided, but not necessarily in equal proportions, into the Parent, Adult, and Child ego states (*What Are Ego States?*, 2021). PAC Model. One thinks, feels, and behaves depending on his/her internal structure. The structural model uses three stacked circles, as explained in Figure 2.

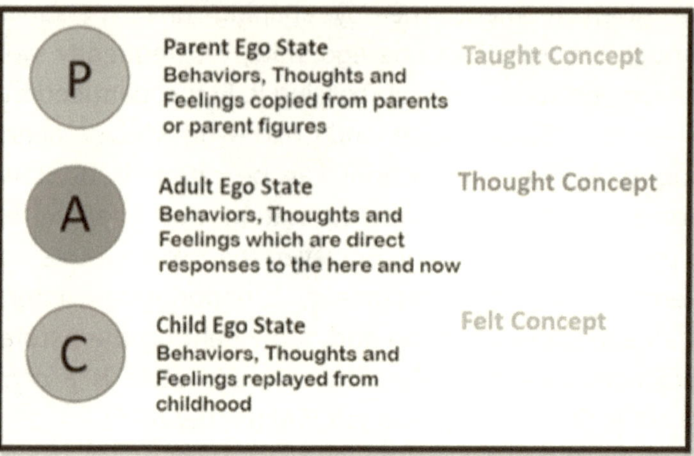

Figure 2: Ego State Model - Structural Diagram (Stewart & Joines, 1987)

Parent Ego State: This ego state is wholly derived from the messages a person receives from his or her actual parent or parent-like figures. When a person adopts a Parental ego state, they exhibit the same gestures, postures, language, intonation, and other behaviours that their parents or parental figures would use. This ego state contains the beliefs, values, and attitudes we have internalised from our parents or other influential figures in our lives. This is our voice of authority, absorbed conditioning, learning, and attitudes. People are conditioned by their parents, teachers, elders, and neighbours (Stewart & Joines, 1987).

Adult Ego State: This ego state is not related to the person's age, but rather to a developmental stage. When a person is in the Adult ego state, he/she is logical and rational when facing reality. The Adult ego state transforms stimuli into pieces of information, processes them, and files them based on previous experiences (Berne, 1961). The Adult takes data from all three ego states, processes them, and makes a logical decision. Adults allow the person to evaluate and validate Child and Parental data (*Description of Transactional*

Analysis and Games by Dr. Eric Berne, MD, 2013). The other ego states can be changed with the Adult ego state (Stewart & Joines, 1987).

Child Ego State: This ego state represents all brain recordings of internal events—feelings or emotions linked to the external events observed by the child during childhood. It is the sum of the senses, encompassing sight, hearing, touch, and the emotional body of data within people. The Child ego is in control when anger or despair dominates reason. Like the Parent ego, we can change it, but not easily (Stewart & Joines, 1987).

To simplify the concept of ego states, Dr. Thomas Harris gave the following equations:

Parent ego is the 'TAUGHT' concept of life.

Adult ego is the 'THOUGHT' concept of life and

Child ego is the 'FELT' concept of life (Description of Transactional Analysis and Games by Dr. Eric Berne, MD, 2013).

6.5.2 The Functional Model of Ego States:

The functional model, also known as the expression model, is derived from the structural model. The functional model illustrates how one applies the concepts from the structural model and how the ego states are manifested in behaviour, thoughts, and feelings (Cornell, 2018). To analyse transactions between individuals and understand the dynamics of communication, the ego states were subdivided, and behavioural descriptions were assigned to them. Thus, the Parent ego state is divided into the Nurturing Parent and the Controlling Parent. The Child ego state is divided into Free Child and Adapted Child (Malhomme, 2024b). Figure 3 shows the five basic Functional Models.

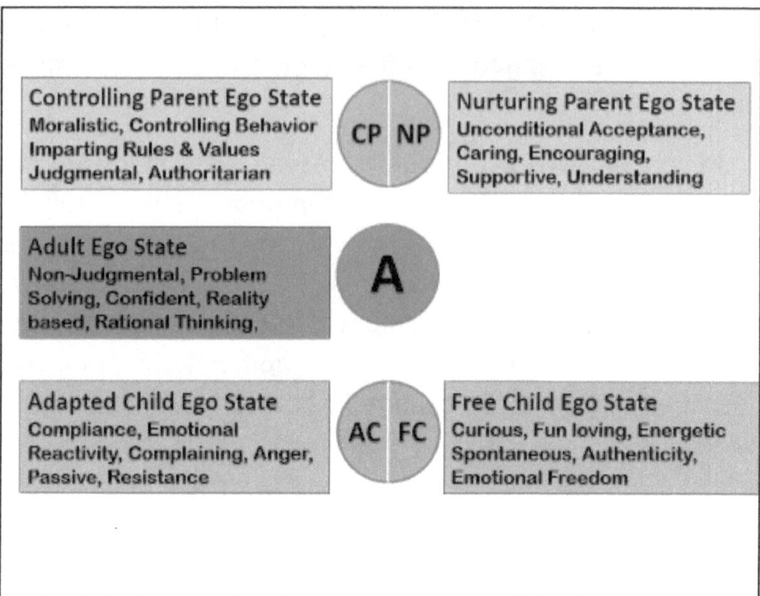

Figure 3: Functional Ego State Model

Nurturing Parent: In the Nurturing Parent ego state, individuals express care, support, and encouragement to others. They make people feel good and comfortable. They appreciate and empower people to be winners (Niwlikar, 2024). For example, when a boss operates from the Nurturing Parent ego state, they appreciate their subordinates for winning a sales contract.

Controlling Parent: In this ego state, a person exhibits controlling behaviour and a fault-finding attitude. However, he can also be organised and moralistic, imparting rules and values to others. For example, a teacher may instruct students to associate with good people.

Adult Ego State: In Transactional Analysis (TA) by Eric Berne, the **Adult ego state** is not subdivided as in the Parent and Child ego states. This is because the Adult interacts with people and their environment in the present moment. The Adult ego state is activated when a person wants to solve problems, make decisions, assume responsibility, or evaluate results. In this ego state, a person remains objective and employs logic, discrimination, and reasoning power. The Adult sees people as they are, rather than what others project onto them. They are not connected with the past but deal with the here-and-now reality. People are cold and emotionless in this ego state. Adults go by information, not assumptions (Cornell et al., 2016). Berne considered the Adult ego state as an autonomous, objective appraiser of reality, interacting with people and their environment in the present moment (Description of Transactional Analysis and Games by Dr. Eric Berne, *MD*, 2013).

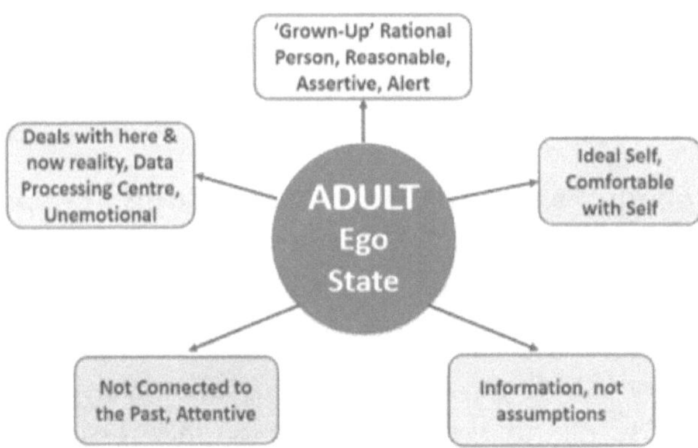

Figure 4: Adult Ego state recreated by Unnikrishnan T.T. based on (*Born to Win: Transactional Analysis with Gestalt Experiments*, n.d.)

Child Ego State: In the functional mode, the Child Ego State can be divided into Adapted Child and Natural Child/Free Child.

Adapted Child: In this ego state, a person complies with the rules or restrictions. They try to please everyone but become depressed when someone criticises their work and feel hurt when things do not go as expected. Most employees remain in the Adapted Child ego state while at work (Stewart &

Joines, 1987). A customer in the Adapted Child ego state will follow the salesperson's instructions.

Natural (Free) Child: In this ego state, a person behaves like a natural child, unaffected by others, disregarding parental rules and limits. The person feels free, spontaneous, energetic, curious, loving, and uninhibited. They enjoy their lives (James & Jongeward, 1996). In the Natural Child, one transacts freely and openly with others. For example, an older man dances joyfully at a party without getting disturbed by others.

However, as people grow up and become adults, they tend to suppress their Natural Child ego state and behave more frequently from their Parent ego state.

The ego states, Controlling Parent and Nurturing Parent, are further divided into positive and negative aspects, as shown in Figure 5.

Controlling Parent-Positive (Structuring): The person in this ego state gives orders, sets limits, and checks if they are respected. The behaviour becomes strict, accompanied by a sharp and rough voice. It adheres to moral principles, facilitating individual integration in the social environment. The rigidity of this ego state inhibits and censors creativity and imagination. Some sports coaches adopt this ego state to get good results (Stewart & Joines, 1987). Some parents behave from this ego state during examination times so that their children do well in exams.

Controlling Parent-Negative (Critical): The person in this ego state underestimates a Child or puts down or discounts the other person. They destructively threaten and criticise others. A person in this ego state attacks others' personalities and behaviour. They drain others' confidence and make them feel they are not OK (Stewart & Joines, 1987).

Nurturing Parent-Positive: A Nurturing Parent-Positive is a parent who helps, gives advice, and looks after their child, respecting their autonomy. In this ego state, the gestures are generous, and the voice is soft and comforting. The conditions become favourable for the child's development, for example, having a supervisor in the company who prioritises employee development (Stewart & Joines, 1987).

Nurturing Parent-Negative (Spoiling): It is an exaggerated Nurturing Parent becoming a hyper protector and blocking the child's natural development. In this ego state, the person becomes over-generous and overprotective. Hyper-protection can suffocate and hinder the child's natural development (Stewart & Joines, 1987). For example, a manager overprotects employees by not giving them challenging jobs due to excessive care for them.

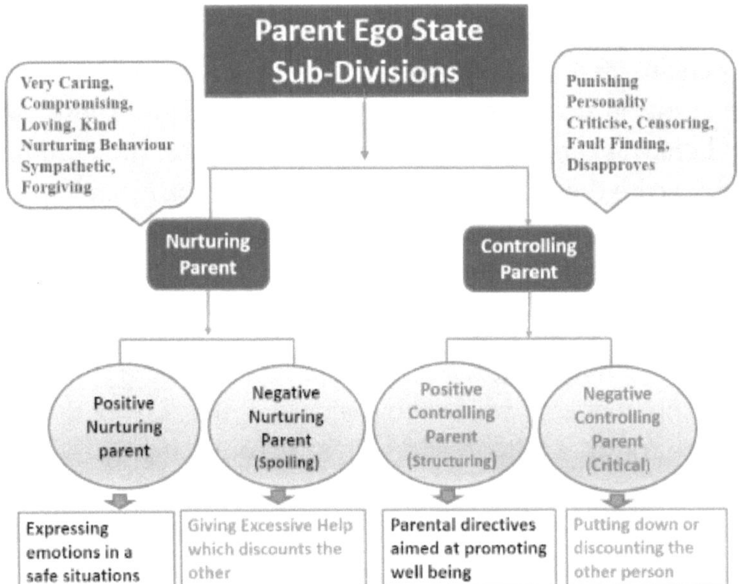

Figure 5: Subdivisions of the Parent ego state recreated by Unnikrishnan based on (Cornell, de Graaf, Newton, & Thunnissen, 2016)

The ego states, Natural Child and Adapted Child, are further divided into positive and negative aspects, as shown in Figure 6.

Natural Child Positive (Spontaneous): In this ego state, a person exhibits behaviours from childhood that disregard parental rules or limits. In the Natural Child, one transacts freely and openly with others. They can be spontaneous, authentic, high-spirited, and curious in a positive way. In this ego state, the person is playful, enjoys life, is open to wonder, and generates creative or unconventional suggestions.

Natural Child Negative (Immature): In this ego state, a person becomes egocentric, impulsive, reckless, immature, selfish, and self-pleasing. They are not concerned about others. They get into uncensored Child emotions, such as a salesperson making inappropriate jokes and laughing uncontrollably during sales meetings.

Adapted Child Positive (Cooperative): In this ego state, a person learns to change or adapt their feelings and behaviour in response to the world around them. These are the behaviours that fit into parents' expectations. They submit and execute the orders received. They accept the group's rules and are quiet, reserved, obedient, cooperative, and friendly. Most grown-ups get into an Adapted Child ego state most of the time.

Adapted Child Negative (Resistant): In this ego state, a person reenacts childhood behaviour that is no longer suitable for an adult situation. They become depressed due to criticism from others at work. Their voices are lively and interrupt communication with others when things do not go their way. The Adapted Child Negative can become the most troublesome aspect of our personality, as excessive docility, fear, and helplessness are the causes of indecision and doubt (Stewart & Joines, 2012).

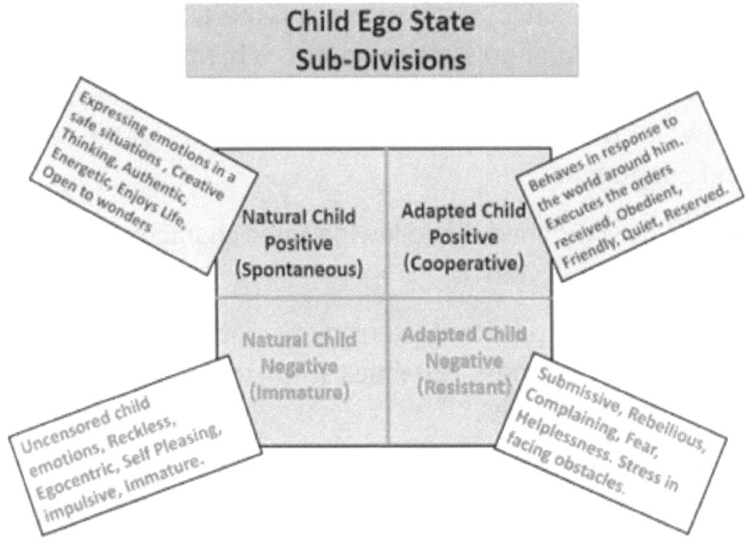

Figure 6: Child Ego State - Subdivisions created by Unnikrishnan based on (Stewart & Joines, 2012).

6.5.3 Integrated Adult Ego State:

Since this book is centred on a sales model based on the Integrated Adult Ego State, I would like to explain it in detail (Figure 7).

As we know, the Adult ego state in TA is not subdivided as it focuses on the present moment, logical data processing, and evaluation of information. One has to develop the Adult ego state for effective decision-making and communication with others. The developed Adult ego state is called the Integrated Adult ego state. This is achieved when the valuable content from the Parent, Adult, and Child ego states is examined, evaluated for relevance to the present moment, assimilated, and integrated into the Adult ego state. This is a person's desired psychological development outcome (Clarkson & Gilbert, 1988). Thus, the Integrated Adult ego state represents a harmonious blend of rational thinking, emotional intelligence, and mindfulness. It allows individuals to respond to life situations with flexibility and adaptability.

Dr. Eric Bern outlined the following three characteristics of the Integrated Adult (1961):

- Pathos: personal sensitivity, attractiveness, and responsiveness (qualities from the Child integrated into the Adult).

- Logos: processing of objective data.

- Ethos: moral qualities and ethical responsibilities (Parental qualities integrated into the Adult). (Cornell, de Graaf, Newton, & Thunnissen, 2016. P 18-19)

In this stage, the person:

i. is entirely in touch with his human potential.

ii. is committed and responsible towards others - characteristics of a good parent.

iii. has the intelligence to solve problems characteristic of an adult, and

iv. can create and express affection, characteristics of a happy and healthy child (James & Jongeward, 1971, p. 299).

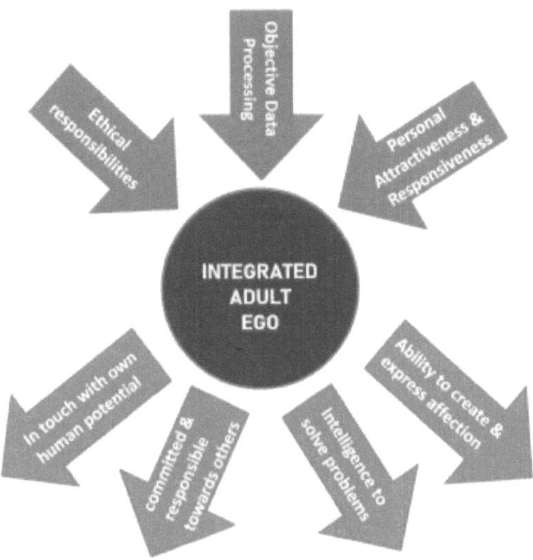

Figure 7: Integrated Adult Ego State, created by Unnikrishnan T.T. on August 15, 2023 (James & Jongeward, 1971. P 299).

Developing an Integrated Adult ego state: Developing an Integrated Adult ego state in Transactional Analysis involves a three-pronged approach:

Decontaminating the Adult from Parental Prejudices: The Parent ego state is a concept taught by parents and stores the attitudes, feelings, and behaviours learned from them or other parent figures. These messages recorded in us may be biased, prejudiced, or harmful. In the decontaminating process, one evaluates the old pattern of behaviour and learns to respond rationally in adult ways. Thus, the person is encouraged to challenge irrational beliefs or stereotypes, develop new coping strategies, create spaces for open conversations, or seek therapy to work through unresolved issues (Finlay, 2015).

Deconfusing the Child's Ego State: The Child's Ego State is a felt concept. This ego state is a repository of our feelings, emotions, and behaviours we experienced when we were young. These can be positive or negative emotions. In deconfusing the Child's ego state, one reflects and analyses past experiences to understand the appropriateness of adult life. Challenge irrational and inherited beliefs. This might involve developing new coping strategies (Finlay, 2015).

Nourishing the Integrating Adult: The Adult ego state is the 'grown-up' self. One can nourish the Integrated Adult ego state by practising being fully present in the moment, making rational and present-focused decisions, seeking objective information before forming opinions, continuously educating oneself, being open to growth and change, and making decisions based on logical analysis rather than emotional biases, and practising mindfulness to improve awareness. This might involve learning new behavioural patterns or cognitive-behavioural techniques to challenge irrational beliefs and develop more adaptive ways of thinking and behaving (Finlay, 2015).

This process takes time. It expands personal capacities for awareness, spontaneity, and intimacy. In practice, an Integrated Adult ego state can be developed.

Thus, ego states become the foundation of Transactional Analysis. Ego state theory in Transactional Analysis is a living, breathing, evolving set of ideas (Cornell & Thunnissen, 2015).

Properly comprehending Ego States helps one discover people's inconsistent behaviour at various times. Thus, it helps us analyse and understand our behaviour and interactions with each other. Therefore, one becomes more responsible.

When a salesperson operates from an Integrated Adult ego state, he becomes open to conversation, rational, less judgemental, and respectful. He listens fully and engages in healthier social interactions. The salesperson analyses the customer's requirements and makes informed decisions. This ego state is helpful for personal growth and effective communication.

6.6 Egogram:

The Egogram was devised by the American Psychologist Jack Dusay, based on the theory of Dr. Eric Berne in the early 1970s (Cooke, n.d.). This test, which consists of a series of questions, serves as a tool for self-awareness. It reflects the personality of the person being tested. The respondent should answer or check the factors that are usually done and are comfortable in their day-to-day life. The results are displayed as a bar graph (*Transactional Analysis*, n.d.). The Adult ego state is in the middle, with Nurturing Parent and Natural Child on either side, as these ego states are more central to a person's self. The Controlling Parent and Adapted Child are placed at the ends, as they are developed under the influence of the outside world. The degree to which a person operates from different functional ego states is graphically represented in Figure 8 (Cornell & Thunnissen, 2015).

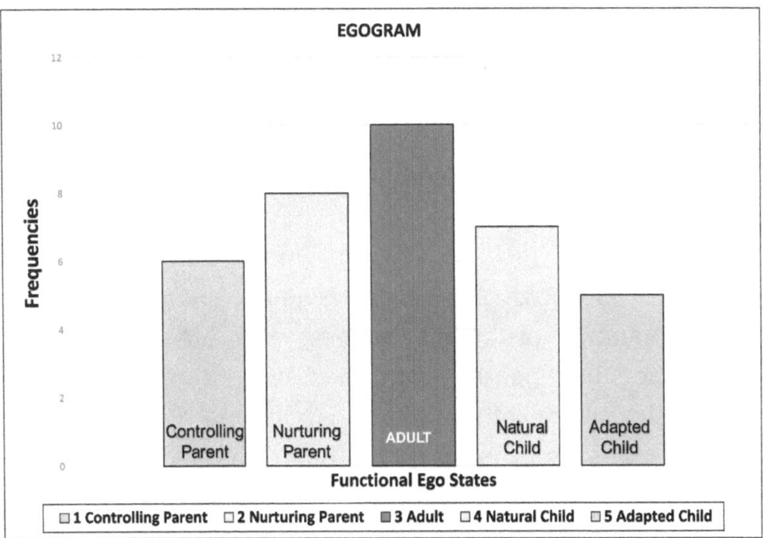

Figure 8: Egogram

As mentioned by Bob Cooke, the bars represent the amount of energy within each ego structure of a person and how they will redistribute the energy among the different egos at a given time (Cooke, n.d.).

This behavioural pattern makes a person both unique and predictable. The precise amount of each ego state is not significant; more important is to consider the size of ego states in relation to one another (Stewart & Joines, 1987, p. 28). The graph of specific ego states is key to understanding one's personality (Cornell & Thunnissen, 2015). Salespersons can analyse their reactions and change their behaviour to improve positive communication. Thus, an Egogram can be used to determine how energy needs to be redistributed by an individual to other parts of the personality to effect a positive change. Egogram helps salespersons understand their behaviour and make adjustments to enhance their communication with customers.

6.7 Transactional Analysis (Proper):

The term "transaction" refers to the fundamental unit of social interaction or communication exchanges between individuals. When people meet, they transact with each other. This can include spoken words, raised eyebrows, expressed feelings, physical behaviours, shared thoughts, stated opinions or beliefs, silence, and other non-verbal cues. When two people encounter each other, one speaks or gestures to the other. This is a transaction stimulus. The reaction from the other person is referred to as a transaction response. The person sending the stimulus is referred to as the agent, and the person who responds is referred to as the respondent. The arrows, known as vectors, show the direction of communication (Murray, 2023).

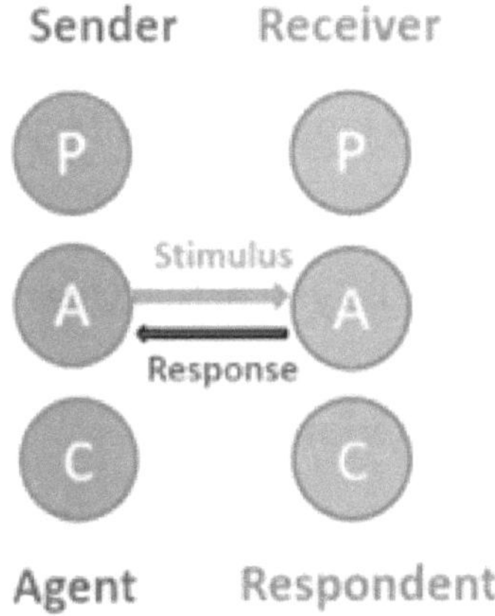

Figure 9: Elements of Transaction
Recreated by Unnikrishnan T.T. Originated by Dr. Eric Berne (Stewart & Joines, 1987)

According to Eric Berne, a transaction consists of a single stimulus and a single response, which can be verbal or nonverbal. It is generally understood that a person transacts from any one ego state (Parent, Adult, or Child) at a time. A person can switch between different ego states during a conversation.

Transactional Analysis is a technique used to analyse the sequence of transactions in interpersonal communications (Murray, 2023). Body language and paralinguistic factors contribute to the meaning of transactions. While interacting, we must be conscious of our feelings, thoughts, and behaviours. When analysing people's transactions, it is essential to consider the accompanying gestures, facial expressions, body posture, tone of voice, words used, and pauses made, to understand the meaning of any transaction (Murray, 2023). By analysing transactions between individuals, we can determine their ego states, and through proper intervention, communication can be made more effective.

It is important to realise that there are three parts to each transaction (2019).

1. What do you say (your activated ego)?

2. What do you expect to "receive?"

3. What response did you 'actually' receive?

6.7.1 Types of Transactions:

Eric Berne defined three types of Transactions (*TA 101 Transactional Analysis Introductory Course Handbook,* 2021).

1. Complementary Transactions

2. Crossed Transactions and

3. Ulterior Transactions

6.7.2 Complementary Transactions:

This occurs when two people's ego states are sympathetic or complementary. This implies that what you say is in harmony with the anticipated and actual responses. A complementary transaction can take place between any two ego states. Thus, a person can transact from his Parent ego state with any ego state of another person. This can be achieved through the use of Adult and Child ego states (Murray, 2023).

Effective Relationship:

Complementary transactions are conducive to building effective relationships with individuals as they facilitate clear communication. The possibilities of conflicts and misunderstandings between people are avoided. In such cases, the lines between the sender's and receiver's ego states are parallel. In short, the communication reaches the desired ego state (Singh, 2022).

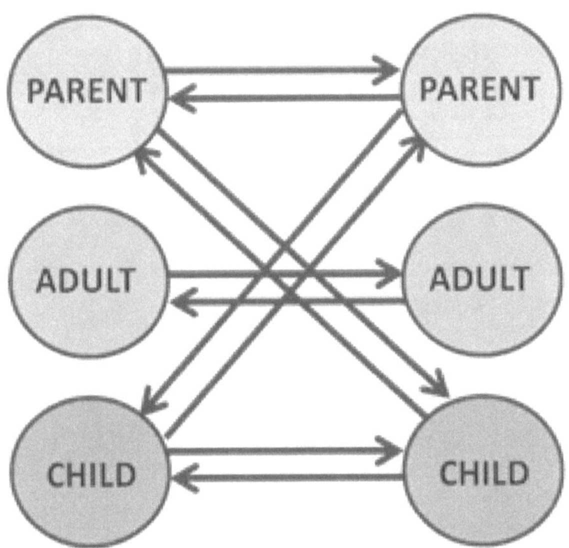

Figure 10: Effective Relationship (Cornell, 2018)

The following transactions are essential for an effective relationship (Cornell, 2018).

1. Parent to Parent: In this transaction, both parties share the same norms and values and can communicate the purpose of life in general.

2. Adult to Adult: Here, thoughts and feelings are expressed clearly and objectively. Communication is open and honest, fostering mutual trust and respect.

3. Child to Child: Communication is emotional and spontaneous. Transactions can be playful, creative, fun, and intimate.

4. Parent to Child: One can be nurturing, providing guidance, instructing, and caring for the other.

5. Child to Parent: One can seek guidance and support from the other. He can learn from others' criticism and instructions.

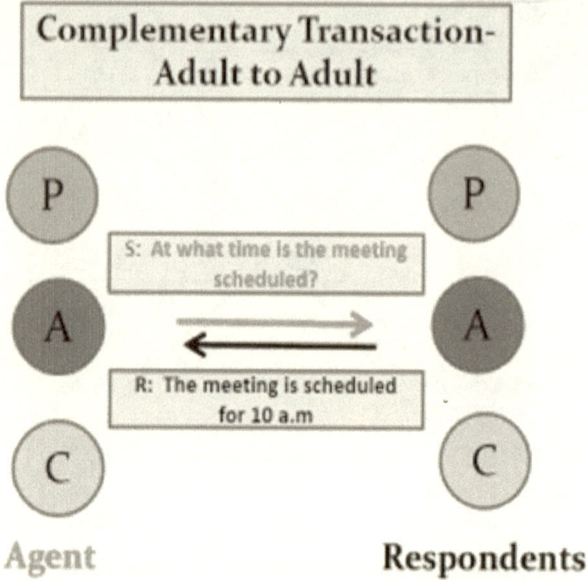

Figure 11: Complementary Transaction between Adult-to-Adult Ego State

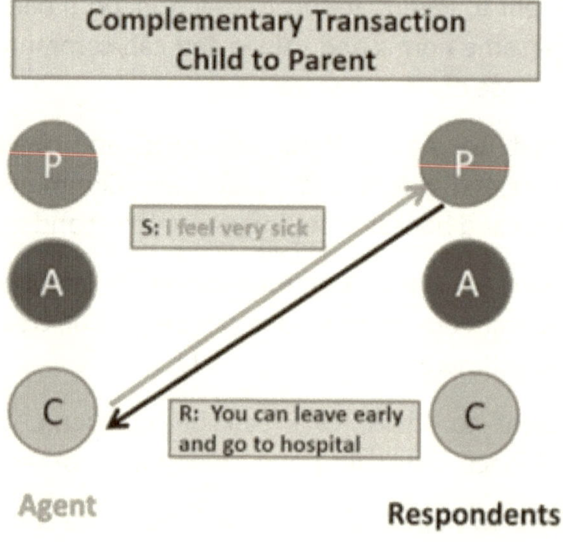

Figure 12: Complementary Transaction between Child and Parent Ego State

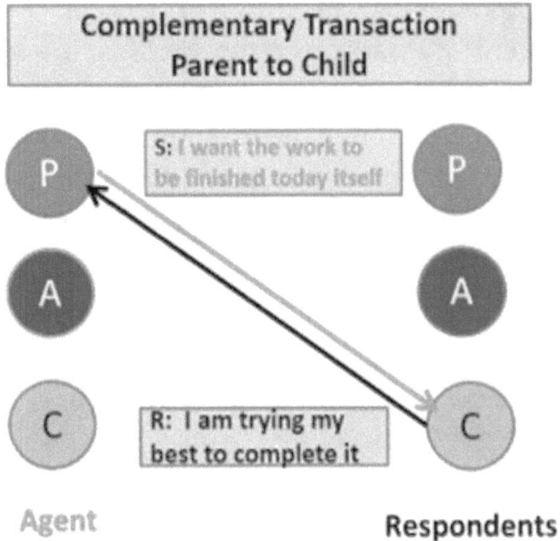

Figure 13: Complementary Transaction between Parent and Child Ego State

We can conclude that complementary transactions significantly help salespeople enhance their communication effectiveness. In such transactions, the communication between the salesperson and the prospect or customer aligns, and the message is understood as expected. The customer feels valued. This will help build trust and rapport, leading to more effective persuasion and improved sales success.

6.7.3 Crossed Transactions:

In a crossed transaction, an unexpected response is elicited by the stimulus. An incorrect ego state is activated, and the lines of transactions between the people are crossed. At this point, people tend to retreat, turn away from each other, or divert the conversation in another direction.

Cross-transactions can lead to discomfort in various relationships, including those between parents and children, spouses, teachers and students, salespeople and customers, employers and employees, and others. A Parent-Child or Child-Parent transaction often crosses an Adult-Adult transaction. Communication is interrupted in a crossed transaction. One person must change their ego state for the continuity of communication. When a conversation gets crossed on the Adult level, the Adult ego state of the conversation partner is reinforced (Murray, 2023).

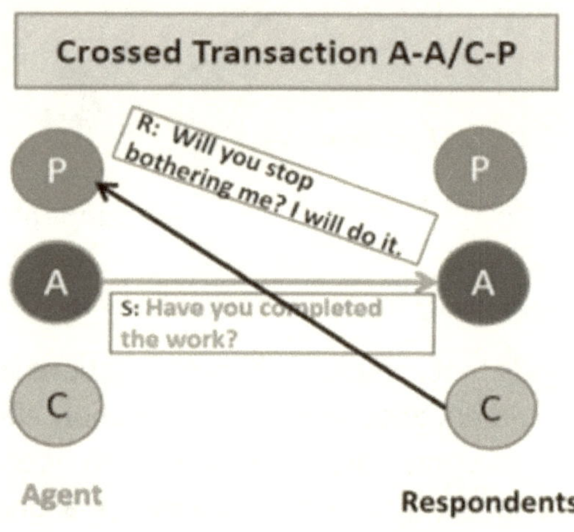

Figure 14: Cross Transaction from Adult to Adult and Child to Parent

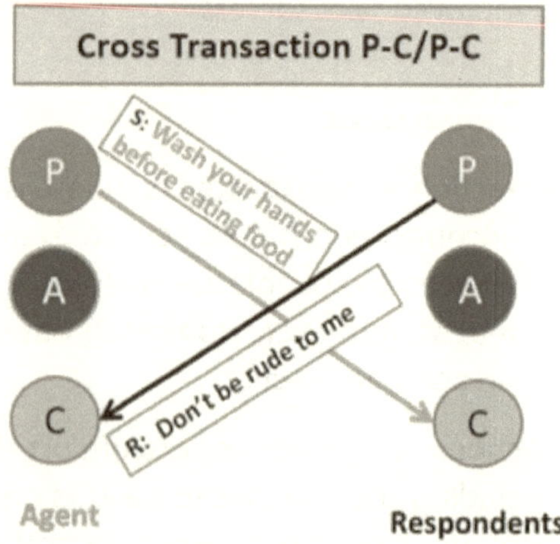

Figure 15: Cross Transaction from Parent to Child and Parent to Child

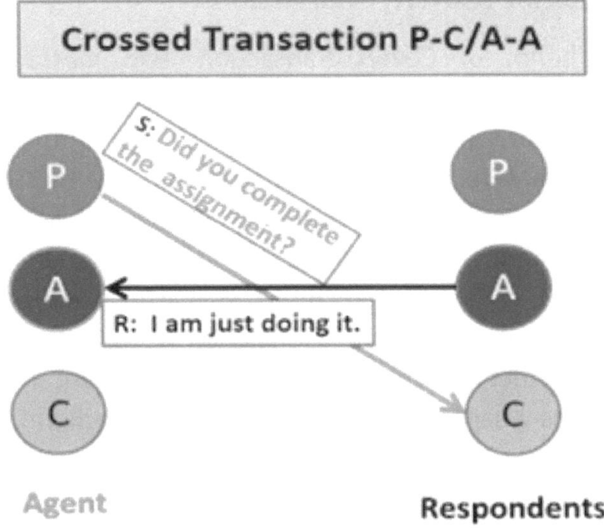

Figure 16: Cross Transaction from Parent to Child and Adult to Adult

It has been observed that when transactions cross, the communication between the salesperson and the customer does not align with the expected outcome. This leads to misunderstandings and conflicts. When crossed transactions with customers become frequent, the salesperson gets emotionally drained. A professional relationship with customers can be damaged, leading to poor performance and failure.

Salespeople should learn to recognise cross-transactions and improve their communication skills. Cross-transactions typically occur when a customer becomes dissatisfied with a purchase and approaches the salesperson for a resolution. Under such circumstances, the salesperson should respond from an Adult ego state. The customer will find it beneficial to arrive at a solution rather than continuing with crossed transactions. The customer, naturally, will respond from an Adult ego state to make the transactions complementary (Adult-Adult), which is healthier and more respectful.

6.7.4 Ulterior (Covert) Transactions:

In an Ulterior or Covert transaction, two messages are conveyed simultaneously. One is an overt or social-level message (words that are said), and the other is a covert or psychological-level message (what is meant). The messages at the psychological level are usually either Parent-Child or Child-Parent. In Ulterior transactions, people have a hidden agenda and do not say what they mean. Sarcasm is an excellent example of this. In sarcasm, the spoken words often convey a meaning that is opposed to the actual intent ("Ulterior Transactions-what's Beneath? - Romasharma - Medium," 2023).

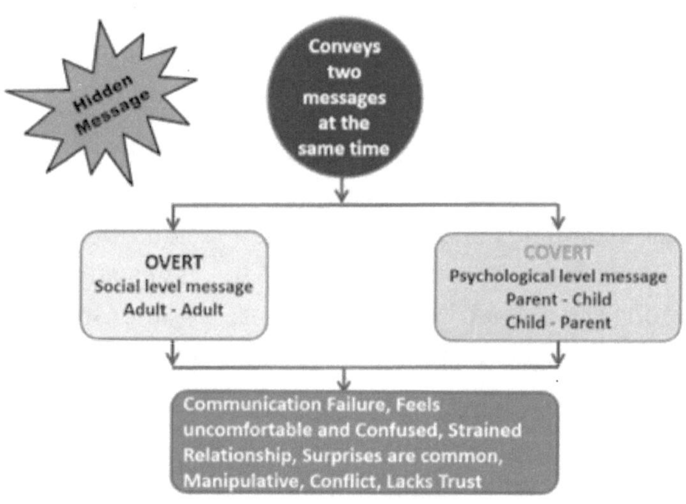

Figure 17: Elements of Ulterior (Covert) Transaction. Recreated by Unnikrishnan T.T. based on (Stewart & Joines, 1987).

Ulterior transactions are often employed by individuals who desire a closer relationship but are hesitant to express their intentions openly. These transactions are manipulative. Such transactions can lead to conflicts and misunderstandings between people. One should be aware of being subjected to ulterior transactions as they are not authentic. Surprises are common. It is better to avoid innuendo and break the conversation down into a set of complementary transactions, exposing the meaning of each step in the conversation. (*Ulterior Transactions: What is Beneath? by Romasharma, Medium*, 2023).

Ulterior Transactions are of two types:

1. Angular Transactions and

2. Duplex Transactions

Angular Transactions: These transactions involve three ego states. The social message is usually A-A, and the psychological message is at P-C, C-P, or C-C ego states. Salespeople, advertisers, politicians, and teachers sometimes use ulterior transactions to convince or persuade others. The stimulus comes from one ego state and addresses two ego states in the other (Cornell & Thunnissen, 2015).

Quoting from my experience: One person came to our office furniture showroom to buy a chair at a low price. He was very particular about the sitting comfort of the chair but was hesitant to pay the price. I made him sit on the top-of-the-range chair. This was a premium chair with numerous features, offering the ultimate comfort level while sitting. The customer felt very comfortable. When he asked the price, I told him, "This is an expensive chair. Would you like to invest in this chair?" After a long pause, he decided to buy and pay for the chair. The Angular Transaction is diagrammatically represented here.

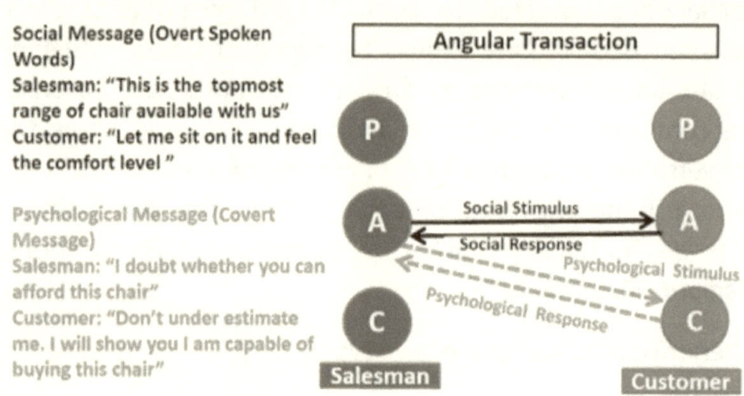

Figure 18: Angular Transactions

Duplex Transactions: In this transaction, there are two different levels of transactions - one at the social level and the other at the psychological level. The social level transaction occurs at the verbal channel, while the psychological level is at the non-verbal channel. Four ego states are involved simultaneously. The ego states are congruent at the social and psychological levels. By analysing Duplex transactions, one can gain insight into their behaviour and communication patterns (Understanding Transactions: Duplex Transactions, n.d.).

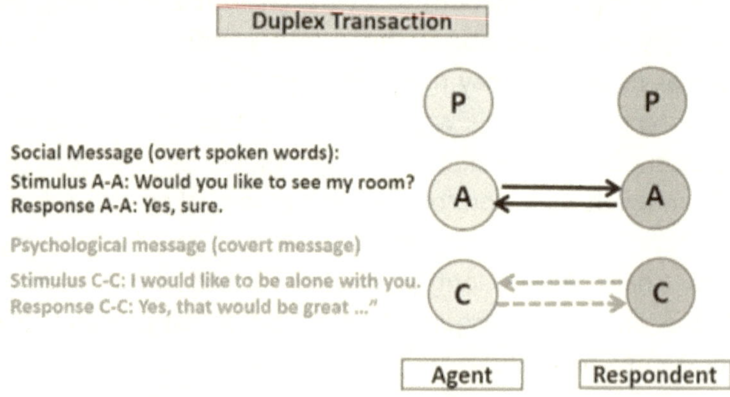

Figure 19: Duplex Transactions (Cornell, 2018)

The salesperson should be skilled in handling Angular and Duplex transactions. They should be able to recognise the covert message (hidden meaning) behind the overt message. Non-verbal messages, such as facial expressions, tone of voice, and gestures, can provide clues about covert messages. Respond to both messages by highlighting the product's features and benefits to the customer, justifying their purchase. The focus should be on meeting the customer's needs. Maintain professional conversation by avoiding the emotional undertones of the hidden messages. Use positive body language throughout the conversation to create interest and understanding in the customer. These methods will help the salesperson understand both covert and overt messages, leading to better rapport and improved sales outcomes.

Specific Forms of Transactions:

Blocking Transactions:

These transactions are used to redefine the situations. People use this transaction when the stimulus is perceived as a threat, they do not want to address a question, or they wish to redirect the conversation. Politicians and journalists use such transactions. A well-known example of a blocking transaction is when a mother asks, "Who here is making a mess?" and the child replies, "Not me!" (Cornell, 2018).

Tangential Transactions:

In this transaction, the stimulus and response address different issues or address the same from a different perspective. Tangential transactions are pretty standard in everyday conversations. When people are in stressful situations, they are likely to redefine the situation. The primary purpose of this transaction is to divert the other person's attention away from the issue that constitutes the threat.

People will likely feel uncomfortable when their conversations go nowhere or seem to go in circles. On the psychological level, this is the intention. Such a conversation can go on for an extended period. Politicians strategically insert tangential transactions to avoid answering questions when they do not want to. For example, during wage negotiations within an organisation, the union representative asks, 'What do you want from us so that we can conclude this agreement?' The personnel manager answered that we were unsatisfied with your proposed conditions. A shift from "wanting" to "feeling satisfied" can be noticed (Cornell, 2018).

Bull's Eye Transaction:

Bull's Eye transaction is the most effective way of communication. The person consciously chooses from their Adult ego state to address simultaneously all three ego states – P A C of the opposite person. The primary transaction is A-A. Usually, the emotions held in the Child ego state are addressed first, followed by the belief system in the Parent, and finally, the thinking and problem-solving of the Adult ego state. The responses from P A C are directed back to the sender's Adult ego state. The Parent ego state creates a value, and C agrees with the process. This facilitates a practical problem-solving approach. (*Bull's-eye Transaction, Role of Transactions in Multiparty Contracting*, n.d.). In this skilful series of transactions, communication remains constructive and balanced, addressing emotional, value-based, and rational aspects of the interaction. Political leaders, sports coaches, and restaurant managers motivate others in this way (Cornell, 2018).

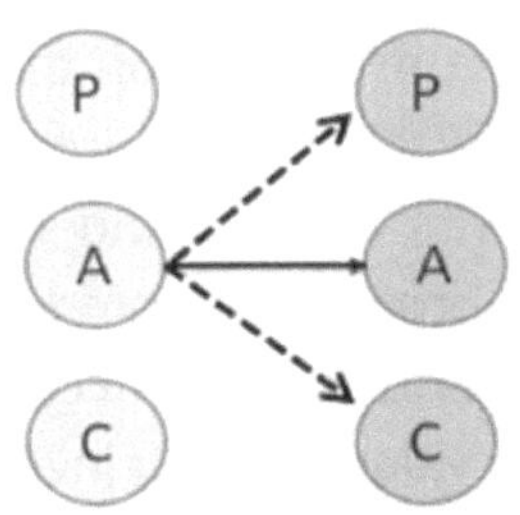

•(S) It's all going crazy! Just when I thought I was on track for promotion, this new young man throws a spanner in the works! I've worked so hard for this! What will I tell my family?

•(R1) [targeting Child]: I can hear your frustration and disappointment...

•(R2) [targeting Parent]: ...and you probably believe that it's unfair for the boss to overlook your efforts...

•(R3) [targeting Adult]: ...how could we begin to think about this to consider some options?

Figure 20: Bull's Eye Transactions (Bull's-eye) *Transaction, Role of Transactions in Multiparty Contracting*, n.d.

Quoting from my experience: In 2009, our company participated in a tender to supply office furniture for a new 10-storey government building. Once the tender was opened, the organisation called the selected vendors for a discussion with a panel of department heads from different divisions. Since our company was a new entrant at the time, I was allowed to present last. When I entered the meeting room, I could see all the panel members looking at me with curiosity, eager to know what I had to offer compared to the established giants.

One of the panel members made a striking remark after reviewing our proposal: "Do you know that your proposal is the highest among all the competitors?" In a pleasing manner, I replied, "Yes, I am aware of this fact." Another panel member asked, "Why so?" I answered, "The answer is simple. One cannot buy Gold at the price of Silver." Though this was a metaphorical expression, it served as a Bull's eye stimulus. I could see the curiosity in the eyes of all panel members.

It was evident that I could address their emotional, value-based, and rational needs. In the Child ego state, they were excited to know what was new. In the Parent ego state, they were concerned with value-based needs, such as the reliability and consistency of the products. In the Adult ego state, they wanted more information on the product features and benefits. Anticipating such needs, I carried all test certificates that proved the products I handled were of high quality. Further discussions convinced them that our furniture was a great value for their investment.

At last, I was successful in getting the order.

Thus, Bull's Eye transactions can be highly supportive of salespersons, as communication becomes comprehensive and engaging.

Carrom Transaction:

Three people are involved in this transaction. One person speaks to another to influence the third person who overhears the conversation. This is common in workplaces. In front of his manager, the boss rebukes a junior employee with a message intended for the manager but addressed to the subordinate to prevent a confrontation or disagreement (Karve, n.d.).

Gallows Transaction:

This type of ulterior transaction occurs when someone smiles or laughs in response to another person's misfortune or failure. The social message may be verbal or nonverbal and is usually polite. The smile or laugh is the psychological message. For example, when a person says, "I am sorry to hear that," while smiling or laughing, it implies that the smile or laugh metaphorically "tightens the noose" around the other person's neck, reinforcing the negative feelings or behaviour. A gallows transaction can be intentional or unintentional, conscious or unconscious, but it is always harmful to the relationship between the two parties (Maxedon, n.d.).

Diluted Transactions:

One part of this transaction is hostile, and the other is affectionate. The message is buried under some form of kidding. For example, a student may ask the other, "Hey Genius, when will you finish that book? I want to read it." The other person might throw the book and remark, "Here you are, butterfingers." Grab it if you can (*Diluted Transactions*, n.d.).

Weak Transactions:

These transactions are superficial and carried out without genuine interest, feeling, or effort. For example, if the wife says to her husband, "I wonder if we should go out for a movie tonight." The husband replies, "It is okay with me. Whatever you say will be acceptable to me" (*Weak Transactions*, n.d.).

Internal Transaction:

This transaction describes what a person may do inside their head or communicate with themselves. It is pretty familiar to all. Each person can shift their ego states and hold conversations between the Parent, Adult, and Child within themselves (Internal Transaction, n.d.).

Quoting from my experience:

Although there are different types of transactions according to Transactional Analysis, the salesperson should learn to select the correct transaction to navigate interactions to their benefit. A healthy relationship comes from healthy communication habits. It is better to be assertive and express needs and feelings clearly, directly, and by setting boundaries. Effective communication requires Complementary transactions free from hidden messages or ulterior motives. With Complementary transactions, the communication continues unless the parties involved decide to stop. Complimentary transactions ensure clear and productive communication. Adult-to-Adult transactions are considered effective and healthy. This is based on information, not assumptions, and hence, deals with reality without unnecessary emotions. However, there may be situations where Parent-Child or Child-Parent transactions are appropriate, which demand comfort and care.

Cross-transactions are pretty common in sales. However, identifying such transactions can help the salesperson avoid conflicts and maintain congenial interaction. For example, if the customer responds emotionally from the Child ego state, the salesperson can switch to the Nurturing Parent ego state to realign the conversation.

Ulterior transactions are also quite common in sales. I have encountered many situations where I made an ulterior transaction to benefit sales. Once we identify the customer's overt and covert needs, we logically address them. This will enable us to establish a deeper connection with our customers. Ulterior transactions can create a sense of urgency to purchase. For example, suppose the salesperson informs the customer about the limited stock availability or a discount that is only available for a limited period. In that case, it creates a sense of urgency to make a purchase. The salesperson may intend to push the sale to meet monthly targets.

By utilising effective ulterior transactions, a salesperson can navigate complex interactions more smoothly and increase their chances of closing a sale.

6.7.5 Rules of Communication:

Berne (1961, 1964) discovered that much communication develops according to the following rules or laws (Cornell, 2018).

1. When the transactions remain complementary, they continue conversations unless one stops them.

2. In crossed Transactions, communication breaks down, and one or both individuals must shift ego states for communication to be re-established.

3. The behavioural outcome of an ulterior transaction is determined at the psychological and not at the social level.

4. In any communication, the value of communication ultimately depends on the receiver and not on the sender.

Quoting from my experience:

I maintain complementary transactions when conversing with customers. This brings magic to our interactions. The conversations became continuous and smooth. The client felt heard and acknowledged. This helped me develop rapport and long-term relations with the customer, which resulted in repeat purchases.

When transactions become crossed, they should be addressed promptly to avoid conflicts. This can be done by changing the salesperson's approach. It is easy to change the salesperson's approach rather than the customer. Understanding the customer's ego states can help the salesperson reframe their conversations for more productive outcomes. For example, a Nurturing Parent ego state can provide reassurance and care to the customer, while an Adult ego state can offer information on product features and benefits. The Child ego state fosters creativity and out-of-the-box thinking, offering creative solutions. Thus, by properly utilising ego states, a salesperson can engage in effective communication to connect with customers, address their concerns, and secure the sale.

6.8 Game Analysis:

In his book "Games People Play" (1964), Eric Berne defined a Game as an ongoing series of complementary, ulterior transactions progressing to a well-defined, predictable outcome (Berne, 1964). The game has a repetitive pattern of transactions with a hidden purpose or gimmick. These transactions are principally intended to obtain strokes, but instead, they reinforce negative feelings and self-concepts and negate the direct expression of thoughts and emotions (Berne, 1964).

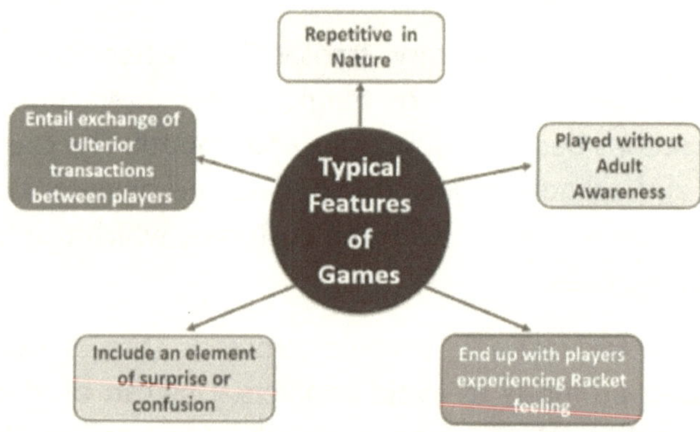

Figure 21: Features of Games recreated by Unnikrishnan based on (Berne, 1964) (*Game Analysis - Transactional Analysis*, n.d.)

The goal of Game Analysis is to analyse human interactions and discover destructive patterns of behaviour to understand the games played and improve the relationship (James & Jongeward, 1971).

Games are played to

- To receive attention and affection, though in a negative way.

- To escape responsibility, commitment, or confrontation.

- To maintain a distance between intimates while still engaging in intense conversation.

- To support one's core attitudes, ideologies, and values.

- To avoid circumstances that could challenge one's views on things (Martin, 2023).

Games played can be identified by

- Understanding the concept of transactions and checking whether interactions take place from childhood anxieties and emotions.

- Identify the ego states and recognise from which ego state the transactions took place.

- Analysing energy shifts. If one person feels their energy drained during an interaction, the other person will be uplifted and energised.

- Noticing recurring patterns in transactions.

- Understanding the other person's motivation and objectives during the transaction. (Tomlinson, 2010)

Quoting from my experience:

I have seen the negative consequences of games. Some salespersons enter the game to manipulate the situation and close the sale, or manage their relationships with customers. They make false promises to save the situation, but they are challenging to fulfil. They play games to fulfil their needs for recognition or validation or to maintain a safe distance from the customers. However, this leads to negative feelings and behaviour, resulting in unhealthy interactions. It causes emotional distress for the parties involved, resulting in frustration and a sense of helplessness. It involves manipulative behaviour and dishonest communication, leading to damaged relationships. This is a bad practice in selling. There is a chance of losing the customer and damaging the organisation's reputation. Ultimately, personal growth will be hindered.

Sometimes, customers play games in showrooms. The customer drops into the showroom, pretending to purchase chairs. They ask for the prices of almost all chairs on display. The customer's intention is not to make a purchase, but rather to test the patience of the salesperson or engage in a casual conversation and pass the time. The customer finally says, "Your products are not very good and are overpriced." The salesperson spends valuable time attending to such customers and gets drained. This leads to frustrations and adverse emotional outcomes as time and effort are wasted.

Salespeople should learn to recognise and address games played by customers. When the customer enters a Game, respond effectively. Ask the customer what they are looking for. Obtain the exact specifications, including the type of chair, details of the upholstery, price range, and expected delivery time, among other details. If the customer is serious about purchasing, they will have a definite answer. The salesperson should be able to set boundaries, striking a polite balance between attentiveness and effectiveness.

6.9 Script Analysis:

A life script is a life plan that is developed unconsciously, based on decisions made during early transactions between parents, parental figures, and the child. For a child, these decisions made sense and helped him to adapt to the world around him. These decisions may not seem sensible when they become adults, but their behaviour is partly shaped by the life plan they established in their early years (Stewart & Joines, 1987).

All humans have an intrinsic desire to connect. The ability to form a bond with caregivers and the desire to form a bond with a child are essential for survival. Thus, in the early stages, a child learns and obeys what to do, see, hear, touch, and feel, and they develop a life script dictated by their parents. This script is carried further in life and ends in a winner, non-winner, or loser (Stewart & Joines, 1987).

According to Dr. Eric Berne, Life Script analysis is crucial for identifying self-limiting patterns and making conscious choices that enable a person to rewrite their narrative for personal growth and fulfilment (Berne, 2010).

This analysis enables individuals to achieve autonomy by identifying the script's impact on their values, decisions, and behaviours (Stewart, 2013). A person becomes autonomous by being script-free (Klein, 2018).

Our Scripts are influenced by (Administrator, 2023).

- cultural and societal forces

- Individual events that emotionally affected us

Script messages are formed in the following ways (Stewart, 2013).

- Modelling: imitating the ways of people around.

- Attributions: The qualities told about a person

- Suggestions: motivation and encouragement.

- Injunctions and counter-injunctions: These come in the form of negative commands.

Life scripts and their effect on (Stewart, 2013).

- How one lives their life.

- How decisions are made.

- The options to make decisions.

- One's self-image.

Quoting from my experience:

While interacting with salespersons, I began to appreciate the importance of life scripts in their lives. Suppose children have been taught throughout the development stage not to talk to strangers, but later, when they become salespersons, they carry the same message in their brains. What will be the impact on their performance? This person will likely struggle with prospecting, a crucial step in the sales process. Moreover, they will struggle to trust others and establish rapport with customers. Anyone who carries the message "I am good for nothing" will hurt their self-esteem and confidence. Negative life scripts can lead to diffidence and underperformance. At the same time, a person with a positive and motivating life script will have the ability to face life's challenges.

However, some salespeople could rewrite their harmful life scripts, overcome their limiting beliefs, and improve their performance.

6.9.1 Life Positions:

"Life position" refers to a person's core assumptions about themselves and others. These assumptions are developed in early childhood and influence interpersonal interactions, communication styles, and overall psychological well-being throughout life. According to TA, there are four main Life

Positions, each expressing a particular confluence of beliefs about oneself and others (Stewart & Joines, 1987).

- **I'm OK - You're OK**: This is a healthy position. This comes from the Adult ego state. In this position, people are willing to trust others with dignity and openness.

- **I'm OK - You're not OK:** This comes from the Parent ego state. In this position, people blame others and put them down to maintain their OKness.

- **I'm not OK - You're OK:** This comes from the Child ego state. In this position, people feel powerless and are primarily depressed.

- **I'm not OK—You're not OK:** This comes from either or both the Child and Parent ego states. In this position, the individual feels hopeless and frustrated, struggling to meet the demands of the world.

Figure 22: Life Positions-The OK Corral by Franklin Ernst, 1971 (2023), (Dmtorbi, 2023)

Quoting from my experience:

Initially, I faced lots of challenges in my sales journey. Although I was passionate about selling, I lacked the necessary guidance and skills to achieve the target set for me. My mindset was not OK, and I struggled with a judgemental attitude, criticising customers without understanding their problems. However, joining the Toastmasters Club and attending counselling courses had a profoundly positive impact on my attitudes, mindset, and behavioural patterns. Toastmasters improved my communication skills and helped me to challenge myself, embrace failure, and learn from it. Counselling courses reshaped my attitudes and behaviour. I could replace negative self-talk with positive affirmations, manage stress more effectively, improve my relationships, and cultivate a growth mindset. All these experiences brought about transformative growth in me, and I was able to adapt to the "I am OK - You are OK" life perspective. This particular life position has helped me in my sales career.

The salespeople who adopt this life position will have the following benefits:

1. They adopt a positive mindset and approach customers with an optimistic and constructive attitude.

2. They believe that all customers possess inherent worth and value.

3. Effective communication helps them to understand the customer and build genuine relationships and rapport. The salesperson actively listens to the customer's requirements and proposes solutions that benefit both parties.

4. Accepting the customers as OK, they feel respected and valued. This leads to customer loyalty.

5. This life position will make the salespersons resilient as they become adaptable and flexible in their dealings.

How do you develop? I am OK. Are you in an OK life position as a salesperson?

1. Analyse your current life position. This can be done using tests such as the Modified Wood test of life position or by reflecting on yourself. It will help you identify your beliefs, biases, or negative judgements.

2. Check whether one gets into the blame game, blaming others for their failures.

3. Replace the negative thoughts with constructive thoughts.

4. Develop social skills by being in a good friend circle that fosters growth.

5. Avoid a superiority complex. People are OK, as mentioned in the philosophy of TA.

6. Develop a growth mindset by embracing challenges. Believe in the fact that we should learn from our mistakes.

7. Develop communication and listening skills to understand customers' perspectives without judgement, thereby balancing the interests of both salespeople and customers.

A comprehensive knowledge of life positions is conducive to promoting psychological well-being, effective communication, and satisfying interpersonal relationships among people. Life positions influence our behaviour and attitude towards self and others. Life positions can be successfully integrated into sales jobs. However, changing life positions is time-consuming. One has to be patient and persistent throughout the process.

6.10 Stroke Analysis:

Berne defined 'stroke' as a unit of recognition or 'any act implying recognition of another's presence' (Lapworth & Sills, 2011, p. 73). All transactions, verbal or nonverbal, are exchanges of strokes. Strokes provide stimulation to an individual. Strokes ideally need to be positive and build self-esteem.

Types of Strokes:

The different types of strokes identified in Transactional Analysis are:

- Positive Stroke: These are expressions of appreciation and pleasant feelings.

- Negative Strokes: These create hurt feelings or resentments.

- Verbal Strokes: These are recognitions and acknowledgements expressed through words.

- Non-verbal Strokes: These are recognitions and acknowledgements expressed through actions or body language.

- Conditional Strokes: These are recognitions and acknowledgements expressed subject to certain conditions or what one does.

- Unconditional Strokes: These are acknowledgements or recognitions given just for being, without any conditions attached.

Depending on the context of the interaction, different types of strokes can be combined to suit specific communication patterns. Transactional Analysis works on changing unhealthy patterns of stroking.

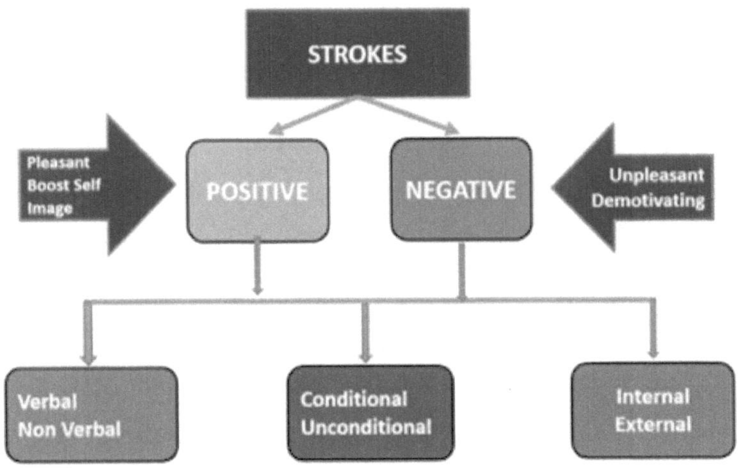

Figure 23: Types of Strokes recreated by Unnikrishnan. (Lapworth & Sills, 2011, p. 73).

Examples of different types of strokes from our day-to-day life are illustrated below:

Types of Strokes	Positive Strokes (Compliments)	Negative Strokes (Insults)
Unconditional (What you are / Being)	"I love you." "I like you." "You're wonderful person!"	"I hate you." "I don't like you." "You're an idiot!"
Conditional (What you do / Doing)	"I like your attire." "Well done on bagging the contract" "You've done a great job!"	"Your clothes look grubby." "I don't like you when you lose an order." "Your work is not at all up to the mark!"

Figure 24: Classification of Strokes (Cornell, 2018).

Selecting the appropriate strokes is important for salespersons to develop rapport with customers. Customers accept such salespersons, which helps build lasting relationships with them.

Quoting from my experience:

'We live by admiration, hope, and love,' said William Wordsworth. This holds in sales. A prospect or customer responds positively to affirmations from a salesperson. During cold calls, when I receive a prospect's business card, I begin the conversation by acknowledging their designation. For instance, I might say, "You are Mr. Alex. It is great to know that you are the Purchase Manager of the company." When there is an opportunity, I provide positive strokes promptly by acknowledging a good decision or expressing appreciation for their decision-making power. For example, "I appreciate your decision to purchase this product," "Your choice is excellent," "This product will help you greatly," and "Thank you for your time." These positive strokes capture the prospect's attention and make sales conversations engaging.

In salesperson-customer relationships, the impact of positive strokes cannot be underestimated. Expressing gratitude to the customer for their business naturally strengthens the relationship. After each meeting, I send a personal email thanking them for their courtesy during my visit to the office. I actively listen and respond positively. When the customer perceives I am thoroughly attentive, the emotional bond and the relationship are deepened.

Strokes fulfil basic human needs for recognition and affection. Positive strokes create positive feelings and enhance the receiver's experience. Recognising and rectifying unhealthy stroke patterns is crucial for building healthy relationships.

Continue Reading... To Satisfy Your Cognitive Curiosity...

Chapter 7

Cognitive Selling

"What differentiates sellers today is their ability to
bring fresh ideas."

– Jill Konrath

Most of us would have observed the changes in the present world. Changing technology, a volatile economy, demanding customers, and tough competition – these have become an integral part of our lives. Experts have been developing innovative selling techniques to thrive in the competitive market. This has necessitated collaboration between Psychology and Sales. The developments in the field of psychology have supported this. Now, we are aware of the mental state of a salesperson, personality traits, social attitudes, customer preferences, and decision-making process. This knowledge enriches the Sales field (Mefteh & Akrout, 2024). The inclusion of psychology in the human decision-making process has led to the emergence of Cognitive Selling. The cognitive selling sales process focuses on the customer and uses psychological insights to get results.

Cognition is the mental process of acquiring, understanding, and utilising knowledge (Neisser, 2014). It involves higher-level brain functions, such as reasoning, attention, memory, perception, imagination, judgment, and problem-solving. These processes comprise a range of interacting skills that enable us to function as healthy adults (*What Is Cognition?* n.d.).

In the cognitive selling sales approach, selling is facilitated by the seller's knowledge and understanding of the customer gained through thought, experience, and senses (Joseph, 2017). This approach focuses on understanding the customer's needs, preferences, and motivations. Through this approach, the salespersons build rapport and trust, create a good customer experience, and increase the chances of making a sale.

7.1 Traditional Selling vs. Cognitive Selling:

Salespersons should possess the necessary knowledge and skills to combat competition effectively in an increasingly competitive market. Knowledge of Traditional and Cognitive Selling approaches will help salespeople formulate effective methods to address the market's challenges.

The differences between Traditional Selling and Cognitive Selling are enumerated below:

Traditional Selling focuses on the product and adopts aggressive sales tactics. It involves manipulations and pressure-filled processes. It is designed to persuade someone to buy, whether they like it or not (Wendling, 2020). Many customers dislike this method and even refuse to meet with the salespeople.

Example: Traditional Selling utilises print media (newspapers, magazines, brochures, etc.), advertising, direct mail, TV and radio, telemarketing, outdoor advertising, and cold calls— contacting prospects without prior appointments.

Cognitive Selling is a customer-focused approach that leverages psychological and neural signals to influence consumer behaviour. In addition to making sales, the focus is on building strong relationships and customer satisfaction. The salesman engages with customers on a deeper level to understand their motivations, preferences, and decision-making processes (*What Is Cognitive Marketing and Why Should You Be Using It?*, n.d.).

For example, using eye-tracking technology to identify the area of the customer's attention, using colour psychology in branding and packaging, creating discomfort to motivate purchase decisions, highlighting potential loss to encourage immediate action, and purposeful personal calls with a customised approach to understanding the prospect, getting emotionally connected, positioning the salesperson as an expert, using reciprocity to build trust, and leveraging cognitive cues for better results.

In today's competitive market situation, both approaches can complement each other. Salespeople exposed to both methods will be better equipped to handle challenging situations, build strong rapport, and achieve successful outcomes.

Quoting from my experience:

I have observed a shift from traditional to cognitive selling over the past few years. I can attribute the following factors to this change:

1. The competition forces businesses to adopt innovative selling methods for survival. Businesses recognised the need to develop a new sales strategy to maximise the utilisation of their resources.

2. In traditional selling methods, salespersons often waste time contacting unlikely prospects. They knock on every door to make sales and experience rejections. This may demotivate salespeople.

3. The digital transformation has changed modern buyer behaviour. They surf websites and educate themselves about manufacturers, products, and services. They prefer to spend less time with salespersons.

4. Buyers expect more. They want personalised services and better interactions without wasting a lot of time.

5. Cognitive selling involves understanding customers' needs and developing a tailored solution.

6. Developments in social media have led to improved communication with potential customers. This supports cognitive selling and empowers sales practices.

In short, competition, customer expectations, time constraints, and developments in social media have contributed to this shift from traditional to cognitive selling.

7.2 Abilities Vs Skills:

In this section, I highlight the difference between abilities and skills. Although these terms are commonly used interchangeably, it is beneficial for a salesperson to understand the difference between them.

Abilities are the talents one is born with or naturally acquired. These capabilities are less malleable. They often relate to the physical or mental attributes of individuals, such as height, lung capacity, and foot size, of an athlete.

Skills involve the application of knowledge, competency, and abilities to perform a task. They are learned or acquired through study and developed or improved over time – for example, public speaking skills.

In the words of Matthew Johns, "Ability refers to the potential or capability of a person to do something, while skill refers to the potential possessed by an individual to do something exceptionally well" (Johns, n.d.). For example, a person can run fast, but to become a champion runner, he has to work at it. Understanding the gap between ability and skill is important for salespersons. This will help a salesperson with self-evaluation to develop existing skills and acquire new ones, thereby becoming more competitive in their field.

7.3 Cognitive Abilities and Cognitive Skills:

Usually, some tend to confuse Cognitive Abilities and Cognitive Skills. These two terms are explained in detail below:

7.3.1 Cognitive Selling Abilities:

Cognitive abilities naturally occur in the brain. They are essential for our daily activities. The cognitive selling abilities of a salesman for his success are listed below:

Active listening: Active listeners remain attentive and participate fully in the conversation. They seek clarification whenever required during interactions with customers. Active listening helps salespersons engage fully in the discussion, understand the needs, and propose solutions to customers (Arootah & Arootah, 2023).

Learning and memory are closely interrelated. Memory is essential for learning (Anderson, 2000b). The ability to learn enables a salesperson to acquire knowledge about product features and benefits, customer preferences, sales techniques, and other relevant information. The memory helps the salesperson retain the knowledge they have acquired. While interacting with the customer, the salesperson recalls the product's price, features, and benefits from memory.

Abstract thinking: This ability enables a salesperson to be creative and consider concepts that are not physically present. It helps solve problems, create new ideas and solutions, and build more substantial and meaningful customer relationships (Abstract Reasoning: Impacts, Examples, and How to Use It— *Calm Blog*, 2024).

Attention to detail: This ability enables a person to examine all task elements, ensuring thoroughness and accuracy when completing the task. This ability allows a salesperson to be more effective. It minimises the likelihood of errors, improving the quality of the task and overall performance (*Cognitive Reasoning: How to Find Candidates with Strong Cognitive Skills*, 2022).

Adaptability: This refers to the ability to adjust one's thoughts and behaviours in response to changing environments. To be more specific, "it is the capacity to make appropriate cognitive, behavioural, or affective adjustments in the presence of uncertain or novel circumstances" (VandenBos, 2007). This ability enables a salesperson to approach customers with an open mind and remain adaptable, ultimately yielding positive results.

Perception: Perception is the ability to capture and process information so that our senses can derive meaning from it (*CogniFit*, n.d.). This ability helps a salesperson to understand the customer's body language, gauge interest during interactions, and tailor their pitch effectively.

Imagination: Imagination helps create mental images and representations, stimulating creativity (Imagination— GoodTherapy.org Therapy Blog, 2015). The ability to imagine helps the salesperson anticipate objections or problems faced by customers and offer creative solutions.

7.3.2 Cognitive Selling Skills:

These are the skills, methods, and strategies that salespersons adopt in their interactions with customers to achieve effective selling. These are learned and developed through practice, experience, and training. Some of the cognitive selling skills are enumerated below:

Prospecting is crucial in sales. This skill helps salespersons identify business opportunities. Prospecting requires a lot of patience. It involves activities such as gathering information on potential customers by keeping their eyes and ears open, conducting cold calls, sending emails, facing rejections, learning from them, and creating a purposeful network to expand the customer base.

Product knowledge: A thorough understanding of the products and services boosts the confidence of the salespersons. Customers prefer to deal with expert salespersons who can clarify their doubts and provide effective solutions.

Language: When we talk about language, four skills—reading, writing, listening, and speaking—are required to express ideas. Strong communication skills enable a salesperson to convey the message effectively, overcome miscommunication, resolve conflicts, and foster teamwork (9 Cognitive Skill Examples and How to Improve Them, n.d.).

Empathy: This is crucial for understanding a customer's emotions and needs. This skill helps salespeople to develop trust and long-term relationships (Brian, 2022).

Resilience: Selling is a challenging profession with its share of ups and downs. Customers may not treat salespeople well, and they may face rejection. They may have to work under pressure. Developing resilience and mental toughness is essential for sales professionals.

Handling Objections: Customer objections are common in sales. Address these objections to convince customers that they receive the best value for their money. Salespersons can prepare for the anticipated probable objections in advance to avoid ambiguity.

Negotiation Skills: Negotiation involves a series of conversations between the salesperson and the customer to reach a profitable deal for both parties. It is stressful and requires preparation, persuasive power, and a willingness to strategically compromise to reach an agreeable deal (Brudner, 2022).

Closing Techniques: Closing is the final step in the sales process, leading to the company's revenue. It helps secure a deal by guiding the potential customer towards purchase decisions, and this skill is vital for sales success (Awesome, 2024).

In conclusion, cognitive selling abilities are inherent mental traits, whereas cognitive selling skills are developed competencies acquired through practice, experience, and training. Sales professionals combine both for their success.

Quoting from my experience:

Attentive Listening:

During my school days, I heard teachers repeatedly telling the students, "Keep quiet," ... "Listen to me." Perhaps that was the teacher's approach to being attentive and listening without getting distracted. It shows that you cannot grasp the subject without listening actively and attentively. Attention facilitates learning.

This principle applies equally to sales. As a salesperson, attentive listening is crucial for understanding the nuances of customer conversations. It is not just about hearing the words; it is also necessary to comprehend the content, meaning, and emotion behind what the customer says.

Once, a customer from an educational institution came to me to purchase 'student chairs.' In furniture terminology, a student chair typically refers to a chair equipped with a writing tablet and a storage basket located beneath the chair. The tablet attached to the chair is for writing, and the basket under the seat is for keeping belongings. Initially, I assumed the customer wanted this type of student chair. However, upon delving into the specifics of the requirements, I understood that he meant a basic revolving chair with castors and no arms. These two chairs are priced differently, the former being more expensive. Therefore, attention to detail is crucial for obtaining the correct product specifications.

This experience reinforced the importance of paying attention to details. To get the correct product specifications, we must actively listen to our customers, understand their needs, and avoid assumptions.

Remember: In sales, attentive listening can make all the difference.

Importance of Resilience in Sales:

In 2014, I lost a sales deal with a multinational company in Bahrain. It was tough for me to accept defeat. I was banking on this sales deal to meet my sales target in two months. My team thought we would secure this deal, as they had put in a great deal of effort preparing the drawing, presentation, pricing, colour schemes, and design elements. Unfortunately, the customer informed me that the contract was awarded to our competitor, as they found their proposal to be superior. My team was upset.

I told my teammates that the customer is right when it comes to selection. There must have been some factors that our proposal lacked. Upon reflection, I identified the limitations of our proposal. The design of our partition system led to compulsive communication among the staff members. This might create noise in the office, and the customer might not be in favour. This was a factor we failed to consider. This oversight proved costly. We lost the sales deal.

However, I did not give up. I maintained regular contact with the company to inform them about our new products and extended our services whenever required. Frequent contact with the various decision-makers helped me build rapport with them. This persistence paid off. I became a familiar face to them. Later, I learned that this multinational company had expansion plans, which would require furniture for approximately 250 staff members within one year. Recognising this as a golden opportunity, we all prepared diligently for the next chance. After a few months, the tender was floated. This time, I was very vigilant. I collaborated effectively with their interior designers and management staff to fully understand their requirements. I made a point to jot down all the key points during my interaction with the customer so that I could refer to them later. Moreover, it exhibited my professionalism and serious participation in the conversation. This record of conversation helped me to frame a proposal accurately. Our revised proposal fulfilled their expectations, providing the following competitive advantages at a reasonable price.

We increased the cubicle height to 160 cm to avoid compulsive communication. This height was suitable to accommodate overhead cabinets suspended on partitions. The overhead cabinets helped the staff to store files, books, and personal items under lock and key.

To make the space more personal, we provided built-in pinboards and writing boards on partitions to display memos, photos, reminders, and notes.

We provided ergonomic chairs with complete adjustments to cater to the diverse health needs of employees.

These features helped employees get organised and improve their productivity.

This time, our proposal had several competitive advantages over other proposals. Moreover, the price was acceptable to them in comparison to the benefits they received. Result… We successfully secured the sales deal.

The lessons I learned are:

1. Setbacks are common in sales, but try to get back. "Crying over spilt milk" will not work in sales.

2. Identify the areas where corrections are needed and make the corrections to achieve better results.

3. Do not give up even when the deal is lost. You lost once, so what? Look for the next opportunity. This world offers us numerous opportunities, but be prepared to seize them.

4. Adopt a progressive mindset. You can rectify your decisions.

Remember, resilience, persistence, persuasion, and continuous learning are key to achieving success.

How did I sell an expensive chair?

In 2007, an insurance company in the Kingdom of Bahrain required 150 chairs. Many dealers, including our company, vied for this order. The insurance company called the shortlisted dealers to understand the offers. Fortunately, I got an opportunity to represent my company and present our proposal.

Preparation and Research:

Why did I propose expensive OK chairs in my offer?

First, I studied the insurance company's official website to learn about its background. I could gather information about the key members of the management team, their financial capacity, and their value systems. They treated their staff well and took care of their comfort. News articles and press releases gave information about their expansion programmes and market position. At that time, the insurance industry was thriving in Bahrain.

I gathered information about the specifications of the chair they were looking for by directly interacting with their representatives. I understood the insurance company wanted to invest in comfortable chairs for better health benefits. I gained a comprehensive understanding of the company's requirements. I proposed OK chairs in our business proposal with the following features:

- Synchro-Reclining Mechanism to provide optimal back support.

- Smart Operations with easy-to-use levers on the armrests.

- Tilt-Resistance Dial

- Height-adjustable armrests.

- Sliding armrests.

- Height-adjustable seat with a sliding facility for seat depth adjustments.

- Adjustable lumbar support (height and depth).

- Five-star leg base.

- Smooth-rolling casters for easy movement of chairs.

- High-quality mesh back and cushioned seat

- Long Durability.

- Choice of colours

I offered a price with a scope for further discounts if needed. This is because people rely heavily on the first information (Anchoring Bias) they receive while making decisions.

Before the scheduled negotiation day, I requested that the insurance company allow me to present on OK chairs. I purposefully asked for this so that I could utilise my public speaking skills. On the negotiation day, I dressed professionally to create a positive first impression - "First impressions last a long time." I maintained good posture and eye contact and used open gestures to convey openness and confidence. I introduced myself and the company I represent clearly and confidently. I presented a PPT on the features and benefits of the chair. Once the presentation was over, the first question posed to me was, 'Your chair is costly.'

This was an expected question from the customer. I have observed the customers posing this question to all the salespeople, even if their products were priced low. They intended to get the maximum value for money.

My answer was that there was always a relationship between quality and price. "Better the quality, better the price". You cannot buy gold at the price of silver. I highlighted the unique features of the chair and the benefits it offered to the customers, including its durability. I told them jovially that this chair would continue to perform even if the user retired from the company. There is no retirement for this chair! I wanted to emphasise how the investment pays off over time due to durability and comfort. Moreover, these chairs come with extended warranties, eliminating the need for expensive repairs or replacements. It saves costs in the long run.

To address their budget constraints, I offered them an additional discount that was safe for my company, along with payments in three instalments over a three-month period. This special offer was available, provided the order was confirmed within 15 days.

The next question was how they could ensure the chair's quality and justify the higher price.

To demonstrate the chair's quality, I physically showcased its ergonomic features. To allow them to experience the comfort level and ease of operation, I invited a few people to sit in the chair and enjoy its comfort. Experiencing the chair firsthand convinced the customer of its worth. This chair had received several notable certifications and awards confirming its functional excellence and durability.

To gain a competitive advantage, I offered to supply chairs in a colour that conformed to their corporate image. This would enhance the company's image and branding, creating a positive impression on its clients and visitors and demonstrating its commitment to excellence.

I created a sense of urgency by highlighting the offer's availability, including additional discounts, instalment payments, and colour schemes, for a limited period of 15 days.

During my presentation, I observed the following clues indicating their interest:

1. They reciprocated positively to my presentation by asking for specific details, such as product features and pricing.

2. They showed interest in checking the seating comfort of the chair.

3. They took notes during my presentation, indicating their interest in my product.

At the end of the presentation, I summarised the key features and benefits of OK chairs, as well as the offers provided, to help them make an informed decision. I said, "I know this chair meets all your needs. This offer is valid only for 15 days. Would you like to take advantage of this today?" They expressed a willingness to purchase the chair but scheduled a meeting with me for next week to discuss further.

The following week, I successfully closed the deal.

Thus, convincing a company to purchase expensive chairs requires a systematic approach that highlights both tangible and intangible benefits, aligning with their values and needs.

In summary, a salesperson's unique cognitive abilities and skills are their best competitive advantage. It is advantageous for companies to employ salespeople with higher Cognitive abilities and skills, as these are strong predictors of sales performance. These salespersons are resilient and work under pressure. They understand the customers better, identify their problems, provide solutions, and thus build strong relationships. Critical thinking and logical reasoning skills enable individuals to make more informed decisions. Thus, companies can build effective and efficient sales teams by focusing on cognitive abilities and skills during the selection process.

7.4 *Cognitive Bias:*

"When dealing with people, remember you are not dealing with creatures of logic, but with creatures bristling with prejudice and motivated by pride and vanity."

– Dale Carnegie

This quote emphasises that people prioritise emotions, biases, and personal pride over logic. Everyone has biases, prejudices, and self-esteem, and they are responsible for their reactions. Understanding these aspects is crucial for fostering positive connections with others.

We often discuss our logical abilities, as they are crucial in various aspects of life, such as decision-making, problem-solving, and scientific research. We associate logical ability with intelligence, maturity, and competence. However, sometimes, our logical ability is compromised by illogical factors. We see that people can be logically illogical. We attempt to be rational but often end up being irrational. Illogical decisions or behaviours arise when emotions, biases, or misunderstandings override logical thinking.

As per scientific research, the human brain takes in 11 million bits of information every second. However, we can consciously process about 50 bits per second (Markowsky, n.d). Since the conscious processing of our brains is small, the vast majority of the information our brain takes in is processed unconsciously. To simplify the processing of information, our brains take cognitive shortcuts. The result is Cognitive bias (*Module 4: Implicit Bias & Microaggressions – Project READY: Reimagining Equity & Access for Diverse Youth*, n.d).

Amos Tversky and Daniel Kahneman introduced the concept of Cognitive bias in their seminal 1974 paper titled "Judgment under Uncertainty: Heuristics and Bias" (Tversky & Kahneman, 1974).

Cognitive biases are systematic and predictable judgement errors we make (Tsipursky, 2020). Many of these come from our evolutionary heritage. As discussed above, these limitations stem from our inherent limitations in mental processing capacities.

There are studies establishing the impact of Cognitive biases on sales.

Matthias Vuorenheimo from Aalto University examined the effect of Cognitive biases on consumer decision-making (Vuorenheimo, 2023).

Showell conducted an in-depth study on how buyer behaviour and cognitive biases affect sales performance (Perez, n.d.). This study found that understanding the interplay between buyer behaviour and cognitive biases is decisive in a salesperson's success.

A survey by Ralph Shad and Ayoolu Olukemi on the Impact of Cognitive Biases on Consumer Decision-Making explains the influence of Cognitive biases on how consumers perceive, evaluate, and make choices about products and services. Understanding these biases enables companies to develop effective strategies that influence consumer decision-making (Shad & Olukemi, 2024).

The above studies show that cognitive biases can benefit both salespersons and customers. When used ethically, a salesperson can establish trust and cultivate lasting customer relationships. This can lead to a win-win situation where the salesperson can close the deal mutually beneficially, and the customers feel satisfied with their purchase.

Types of Cognitive Biases:

Some of the Cognitive biases that influence the salesperson's and buyers' decision-making processes are detailed below:

Anchoring Bias: "Anchoring Bias is deeply rooted in our brain functioning and occurs when we rely heavily on the early information we receive in a decision-making process." (Brontén, 2021).

This is quite common in business. Sellers typically set a high initial price for their products, which anchors prospective customers' thoughts. Later, the price is reduced by offering discounts. The discounted price seems attractive, and the customer believes they got a good deal because of the higher anchor. Anchoring Bias can strategically influence purchase decisions and attract more business.

Confirmation Bias:

The English psychologist Peter Wason first described the concept of confirmation bias in the 1960s (MSEd, 2024). He demonstrated that people tend to seek information that confirms their existing beliefs (Wason, 1960).

Salespersons with a confirmation bias tend to favour information that confirms their existing beliefs about the situation. They do not challenge their existing belief. Most probably, they ignore other information. For salespersons, this bias may lead to misjudging prospects, overconfidence, and an incomplete understanding of their actual needs.

Customers with confirmation bias also favour information that confirms their existing beliefs.

This bias may lead customers to form an incorrect perception of the product, resulting in ineffective interactions with salespeople and incorrect decisions (Multiplier, n.d.).

Hindsight Bias:

"Hindsight bias occurs when people feel that they 'knew it all along,' that is, when they believe that an event is more predictable after it becomes known than it was before it became known" (Roese & Vohs, 2012). It is pretty standard to hear phrases like "I told you so," which predict the outcome of an event after it has occurred. It shows they knew the final result before it happened.

Hindsight bias can significantly impact salespersons, making them overconfident in their predictions and leading to distorted learning and misjudgements of customer behaviour. All of these will negatively impact team dynamics.

Availability Heuristics:

Amos Tversky and Daniel Kahneman, in their seminal 1974 paper, "Judgment under Uncertainty: Heuristics and Biases," defined heuristics as mental shortcuts or rules of thumb that simplify decision-making processes, especially under conditions of uncertainty (Tversky & Kahneman, 1974). Under the Availability Heuristic, people make decisions based on readily available information, which can lead to systematic errors in judgement. This can affect a salesperson in the following way: If a salesperson sells a large quantity of a particular model product to a new customer, they may try to aggressively push the same model, as they believe it has high demand. This is because they were able to recall their recent experiences more efficiently. Due to this, they may not focus on other models. This leads to biased decisions as the salesperson may not consider the market trends or customer preferences.

Cognitive Dissonance:

Leon Festinger defined Cognitive dissonance as a psychological state resulting from two or more contradictory cognitions, such as beliefs, attitudes, or behaviours (Festinger, 1962). These conflicting cognitions create uncomfortable tension in people. They try to reduce the tension by altering their cognitions to achieve consistency (McLeod, 2023)

Cognitive dissonance can significantly impact both salespeople and customers in various ways.

A salesperson may face cognitive dissonance when asked to sell a product they do not believe in. For example, a nonsmoker who personally believes that smoking is injurious to health may be forced to sell cigarettes, or a salesperson may feel they sell products to meet the sales targets even though they are not the best fit for the customer. If a salesperson feels that they are compromising their integrity, it leads to job dissatisfaction and feelings of guilt. This may negatively affect their sales performance and damage customer relationships.

Customers may face cognitive dissonance when they realise that the products they purchased do not meet their expectations or receive damaging information about them. They may seek information to justify their purchase decision. Too many options or exposure to conflicting reviews will complicate the buying process for customers. Dissatisfied customers may spread negative comments about the products and the company, which can tarnish both the product's and the company's image.

Addressing the cognitive dissonance between salespersons and customers is important for the organisations.

For salespeople, it is important to

- Provide accurate and transparent product details to avoid ambiguity in the future.

- Stay in contact with the customer after the sale to address any concerns or questions they may have.

- Highlight the positive aspects of the products to reconfirm customers' beliefs regarding their purchase decisions.

- Address the issues that may arise promptly to resolve conflicting thoughts.

- To provide warranty or after-sales service to make customers confident about their purchase.

For customers, it is important to:

- Be clear about the product features, benefits, and limitations. This will help the customers to be realistic and reduce post-purchase dissonance (Pillai, 2021).

- Seek more information about the products purchased if you are uncertain after making a purchase.

- Focus on the key features of the products and their potential benefits.

- Discuss the purchase among your circle of friends to gain support.

It is common for companies selling expensive products to design a marketing campaign to create awareness of their products' competitive advantage. They try to justify their high prices through such campaigns to resolve conflicts about high prices (*What Is Cognitive Dissonance in Sales? (Explained With Examples)*, n.d.).

Addressing cognitive dissonance can help salespeople build stronger customer relationships, benefiting both parties.

The Egocentric Bias:

In Egocentric bias, individuals overemphasise their perspective and significance in events and interactions. It distorts individuals' perception and memory to enhance their importance. It operates universally and unconsciously, causing us to view life through a self-centred lens (Scribbr, n.d.). For example, a salesperson who is overly enthusiastic about a product's aesthetic appeal might assume that all customers will share the same excitement about it. As a result, in their sales conversations, they focus on aesthetic appeal and fail to explain the other features and benefits that customers look for.

Egocentric bias can significantly impact both salespersons and customers in various ways:

Egocentric bias makes salespeople:

- Assume that customers are equally knowledgeable about the product and skip essential information that is beneficial to them.

- Miscomprehend the customers' needs, as the salespersons assume that what appeals to them will equally appeal to customers. As a result, salespersons' recommendations will not align with customers' requirements, leading to a loss of sales.

- They may develop overconfidence in their ability to convince customers, resulting in less preparation and adaptability in sales interactions (Johnson, 2022).

Egocentric bias makes customers:

- Overestimate their knowledge and understanding of a product, leading to poor purchasing decisions. They mistake a salesperson's enthusiasm for genuine product quality rather than recognising it as a sales tactic (Scribbr, n.d.).

- Overvaluing their past experiences and preferences. This causes them to overlook new information or alternative products that might better suit their needs (*The Egocentric Bias: Why It's Hard to See Things From a Different Perspective*, n.d.).

- Lose the ability to appreciate the value of products that don't match their beliefs or preferences. This can lead to decision paralysis or suboptimal choices (*The Egocentric Bias: Why It's Hard to See Things From a Different Perspective*, n.d)

It can be concluded that overcoming egocentric bias is necessary to improve salesperson-customer interaction. Some strategies to mitigate this bias are listed below:

For Salespeople:

- Encourage salespeople to develop self-awareness through self-reflection to identify their biases (*The Egocentric Bias: Why It's Hard to See Things From a Different Perspective*, n.d.).

- Train the salespeople to practice active listening. This will help them fully concentrate, understand, respond, and remember customers' discussions. Salespersons learn to focus on the customers' requirements (Balto, 2022).

- Establish a proper system for monitoring customer and peer feedback. This will help pinpoint areas influenced by egocentric bias (*The Egocentric Bias: Why It's Hard to See Things From a Different Perspective*, n.d.).

For Customers:

- Encourage open communication with customers to ensure they feel comfortable discussing their needs and concerns. This will reduce misunderstandings (Balto, 2022).

- Provide clear and comprehensive information about the products and services. This will help them make informed decisions without bias.

- Offer educational resources to customers to understand the sales process and the importance of considering alternatives (*The Egocentric Bias: Why It is Hard to See Things From a Different Perspective*, n.d.).

- Encourage customers to give regular feedback on the products and their experience. This will help them understand their biases and their effects on their interactions (Balto, 2022).

Thus, overcoming egocentric bias enables companies to formulate rational strategies that understand and fulfil customer preferences. This will lead to stronger customer relationships and increased sales.

Actor-Observer Bias: Social psychologists Edward E. Jones and Richard E. Nisbett introduced the concept of this bias in 1971 (Jones, 1971). According to this bias, "people tend to attribute their actions to external, situational factors while attributing others' actions to internal, dispositional factors" (MSEd, 2023). This bias occurs when facing failures (*Social Psychology*, n.d.).

When one faces failure, this bias becomes more evident. People usually blame others for their failures. However, when others face failures, we blame them for their actions, leading to inaccurate judgements (MSEd, 2023).

When salespersons lose an order or fail to close a sales deal, they may blame external factors such as market conditions, high prices, or low quality. However, the sales supervisor might think that failure is due to internal factors, such as the salesperson's non-competence or incorrect approach (Nikolopoulou, 2023).

At the same time, when salespersons successfully close a deal, they often attribute it to internal factors such as skills, competencies, and personal efforts. However, the sales supervisor might attribute the success to external factors, such as favourable market conditions, competitive pricing, and high product quality. I have observed some sales supervisors making such remarks - "The salesperson did not sell the product, but the customer bought the product from the salesperson." Such remarks demotivate the salespersons as their efforts and skills are undermined.

Ways to Mitigate Actor-Observer Bias:

a. Encourage salespeople to regularly reflect on their behaviour and consider how external factors influence their actions. Pause before making quick judgements and think about possible reasons. For example, if a customer is non-cooperative or indifferent, check whether they are undergoing personal problems or stress (Calm Editorial Team, 2024).

b. Train salespersons to practice empathy, understanding customers' perspectives and challenges (Calm Editorial Team, 2024).

c. Check whether the salespeople suffer from biases and unfairly judge customers. In such cases, it is important to overcome biases first.

d. Focus on solving problems and not blaming others. Blaming others wastes energy; instead, focus on finding solutions to improve the situation (Rice et al., 2021).

e. During sales meetings, discuss how external factors such as market conditions, competition, customer preferences, and product availability can affect sales outcomes (Scribbr, 2022).

Implementing the above strategies to improve teamwork and customer interaction can help the sales team develop a more balanced approach.

Self-Serving Bias:

Morris Rosenberg, a social psychologist, identified the concept of self-serving bias in 1965 (Calisaan, 2023). Self-serving bias is the tendency for individuals to attribute their success to their abilities and failures or adverse outcomes to external factors, such as bad luck or unfavourable situations (Calisaan, 2023). People adopt this bias to protect their self-image.

This bias impacts salespeople both positively and negatively. Notably, it helps salespeople maintain high self-esteem and confidence, which catalyses their high performance, as they view success as a result of their skills and efforts (Bergland, 2023). Their belief in their abilities prompts them to exert more effort, thereby increasing their motivation to perform well.

Negatively, it does not allow salespersons to learn from their mistakes and improve their abilities, as they attribute failures to external factors. This may lead to conflicts within the team as the team members avoid responsibility. The strained relationship leads to unethical behaviour (BetterUp, 2023).

Overcoming the self-serving bias is crucial in sales for personal growth, enhanced learning, and improved team dynamics. This bias can be reduced by

- Analysing the successes and failures to understand the role of internal and external factors.

- Gaining constructive feedback from peers and managers to get a balanced perspective on performance.

- Looking at challenges as an opportunity to learn, not a threat to self-esteem.

- Sharing experiences to learn from each other by appreciating others' contributions and rectifying our mistakes.

- Regular coaching sessions to help salespeople identify and address their biases. Qualified mentors can share their experience and knowledge to overcome similar biases (BetterUp, 2023).

Recognising and addressing this bias enables salespersons to have more balanced self-assessments, healthier interpersonal relationships, and a more constructive and supportive work environment.

The Dunning-Kruger Effect:

The psychologists David Dunning and Justin Kruger described this phenomenon in 1999 (Wikipedia contributors, 2024). This is a cognitive bias in which individuals with low ability or knowledge in a specific area are unaware of their limitations and overestimate their competence (MSEd, 2024).

This can significantly affect salespersons with low ability as they overestimate their competence. They resist further training, hindering their personal growth. Since they are overconfident, they try to dominate discussions and decision-making processes, sidelining more competent team members. Skilled members often become frustrated or demoralised. Ultimately, this results in overpromises, which negatively impacts the quality of work and customer relationships (Team, 2024).

The simplest way to overcome the Dunning-Kruger effect is to gain more knowledge and experience about the subject. The following measures will be helpful to overcome this effect (Mind Help, n.d.):

a. Question our knowledge instead of unquestioningly accepting our opinions and claims to determine whether we are going wrong.

b. Critically analyse our skills and knowledge to assess them and make a rational decision.

c. Continuous learning and practice will lead you to a deeper understanding of the subject. One can deepen our understanding by reducing the gap between our actual and perceived competence, overcoming the Dunning-Kruger Effect.

d. Accepting both positive and negative feedback is essential for growth. Honesty is essential in accepting criticism, as it demonstrates our willingness to improve. Instead of rejecting criticism, investigate it and focus on self-improvement.

e. Constructive criticism from seniors or experienced staff helps us identify our areas for improvement. This will foster awareness and realistic confidence. Feedback can provide valuable insights into one's competence.

Optimism Bias:

Psychologist Neil Weinstein first described the optimism bias (Weinstein, 1980, p. 810). This bias causes people to believe that they are less likely to experience adverse events and more likely to experience positive events than others. With this bias, people tend to underestimate potential risks and challenges, which can impact their decision-making.

Optimism bias can significantly impact salespersons in both positive and negative ways. Here are a few key effects (HubSpot, 2024).

a. With an Optimism bias, salespersons will tend to be overly optimistic about their sales prospects. This helps them stay persistent in the face of rejection. Their enthusiasm makes them more energetic and engaging with potential customers.

b. Salespersons confidently set unrealistic targets that are difficult to meet. This will lead to disappointment.

c. Salespersons may underestimate the difficulties and challenges, leading to inadequate preparation for sales efforts.

d. Salespersons are encouraged to take risks and pursue high-reward opportunities, hoping to get the sales deal. If they succeed, it will be beneficial; otherwise, they will be disappointed.

e. With an Optimist bias, salespersons make tall promises that are difficult to fulfil, leading to customer dissatisfaction. At the same time, salespersons' optimistic attitudes help them build strong customer relationships.

The following strategies help salespersons to overcome Optimism bias:

a. Think logically and objectively, evaluating both the positive and negative aspects to gain a balanced perspective. Consider the risk factors associated with each decision (*Optimism Bias*, 2024).

b. Learn from negative consequences or others' failures. This will prepare one to face future unpleasant or surprising events (*Optimism Bias*, 2024).

c. Consult with experienced and knowledgeable individuals to gather diverse perspectives and make informed decisions (*Optimism Bias*, 2024).

d. Keep track and regularly review all assumptions to identify and adjust overly optimistic assumptions (*4 Ways to Tackle Optimism Bias*, 2023).

e. Remember unpleasant past experiences to make sensible decisions in the future. Do not repeat the same mistake (*Optimism Bias*, 2024).

The Framing Effect:

Psychologists Amos Tversky and Daniel Kahneman introduced this. In this bias, people tend to choose options based on how they are presented, whether positively or negatively (Perera, 2023). Our impression of an item depends upon (Yashinsky, 2023):

- The content of the presentation

- The tone in which the message or information is conveyed to us

- How are the words or phraseology used for explanation?

For example, the message "Save $100 a year by using energy-efficient appliances" (gain frame) will have more impact on prospects than the message "Lose $100 a year by not using energy-efficient appliances" (loss frame) (Perera, 2023).

The Framing Effect influences sales and marketing, depending on the presentation of information. Some of the positive and negative impacts of this bias are detailed below (Roguska, 2023).

The Framing Effect is a powerful tool in sales and marketing, where the way information is presented can significantly influence decision-making. Here are some ways a salesperson can use the Framing Effect to boost sales:

a. It helps to highlight the product's benefits, appealing to customers' cognitive needs. This means it appeals to the mental processes involved in gaining knowledge and understanding about the product. This helps in decision-making.

b. Products can be made more attractive by visual framing using high-quality pictures and videos to make the product benefits more tangible.

c. Messages can be framed to avert loss by informing the customers about the validity of special offers for a limited period.

d. Framing a message, including customer testimonials, will make the product more reliable as the users will have first-hand experience with it.

However, the Framing Effect can negatively impact salespersons, though it has potential benefits (Vinney, 2024):

a. If the Framing Effect is used to manipulate customers' decisions, it can lead to a loss of trust, damage the salesperson's reputation, and result in the customer's loss.

b. Under the Framing Effect, if salespersons concentrate on information presentation rather than the product's value, customers feel misled when the product falls short of expectations.

c. Highlighting only the positive aspects and benefits while concealing the negative aspects can raise ethical concerns. Customers may feel deceived, which may lead to legal problems.

d. It is quite possible that Framing may boost short-term sales, but it may damage long-term relationships.

From the above, it is pretty evident that overcoming the Framing Effect is important for salespersons to:

Become more rational to improve decision-making.

Present information transparently.

Sell ethically.

Retain customers, build better customer relationships, and effectively sell.

Overcoming the Framing Effect:

Salespersons can overcome the Framing Effect by adopting the following steps (Hoffman, 2024):

a. Create awareness and knowledge about the Framing Effect through training sessions and workshops.

b. Critical thinking and analysis of the options presented to the customers.

c. Present information transparently without bias, using a balanced frame that shows both positive and negative aspects to provide a complete picture.

d. Through open dialogue and critical assessment of the situation in the organisation.

e. Overcoming the Framing Effect helps the salespeople be authentic in their presentations of the products and services. The client makes informed decisions, which leads to better customer relationships.

Cognitive biases are natural and affect most of us. We can mitigate their effects by gaining awareness about their triggers and impact. This requires continuous practice, perseverance, and patience, but it is ultimately rewarding.

7.5 Cognitive Biases - A Powerful Tool for Selling!:

Cognitive biases can be a powerful tool for salespeople to influence customer behaviour to their advantage and increase sales. However, exercise these strategies ethically and responsibly.

Some of the cognitive biases that can be used ethically to enhance sales are listed below (Blaess, 2024).

a. Social Proof: It is natural for people to look to others before making decisions, especially in uncertain situations. Testimonials, reviews, and case studies serve as social proof, showing that users have positive experiences with the product. This can influence potential users' purchasing decisions. This is primarily practised in the hotel industry, where guest reviews are used to convince potential customers about the comfort and security of their stay.

b. Scarcity Effect: Normally, people value items perceived as scarce. In most cases, messages emphasising limited availability or offers valid for a short period create a sense of urgency to purchase the product.

c. Anchoring Bias: When making decisions, people often rely too heavily on the first piece of information they receive, known as the "anchor." Sellers can set a high initial price to make subsequent offers seem more attractive. For example, if a product is initially priced at $1000 and then offered at a discounted price of $700, potential buyers perceive it as a better deal.

d. Reciprocity: People feel obliged to return favours received from others. When businesses offer free samples or something of value to potential customers, it can create a sense of obligation to reciprocate by purchasing the product.

e. Authority Bias: People tend to trust the opinions or recommendations of individuals perceived as authoritative or trustworthy, regardless of the authenticity of those opinions or suggestions. Businesses use experts or celebrities to promote their products, thereby increasing sales. For example, dentists promote toothpaste.

f. Bandwagon Effect: This effect prompts people to purchase products because others are doing so, regardless of their personal preferences or beliefs. People tend to follow the trend. Businesses use this effect to boost their sales by creating an image that their products are widely accepted and trusted. This is particularly prevalent in the fashion industry, where individuals adhere to a specific style or fashion trend.

g. Loss Aversion: People typically prefer to avoid a loss rather than gain something of equivalent value. This means the pain of losing is more than the pleasure of gaining (Nickerson, 2023). Businesses capitalise on this bias by offering warranties on their products, money-back guarantees, or free trials, thereby making customers feel more at ease.

h. Halo Effect: According to this cognitive bias, when we perceive an individual, company, or product positively in one area, we are likely to assume they positively influence other areas even without evidence to support this. Businesses utilise the halo effect by focusing on one positive aspect, thereby changing the overall perception and promoting their products. For example, attractive packaging is used to convey the perception that the product is of higher quality.

i. Mere Exposure Effect: According to this bias, people tend to develop product preferences due to familiarity with them. The more we are exposed to a product, the more the chances of liking it (Nickerson, 2023). Businesses make their products familiar to the target audience through repeated exposure via advertisements, email marketing, social media, and other channels.

j. The Bizarreness Effect: According to this effect, humans remember strange, unusual, or bizarre information more quickly than standard facts and figures (Bizarreness Effect Definition | Psychology Glossary | AlleyDog.com, n.d.). This is mainly because we are interested in novel, strange, or unusual information. This effect can be used to promote products by creating memorable advertisements, storytelling, highlighting unusual product features and benefits, and making products distinct to stand out from the crowd.

k. The Empathy Gap: In this cognitive bias, people find it challenging to understand mental states that are different from their present state or how they affect people's judgment and decision-making (The Empathy Gap: Why People Fail to Understand Different Perspectives, n.d.). This bias can be used effectively in sales by understanding and addressing customers' emotional states. For example, if a customer is dissatisfied or frustrated, acknowledge their dissatisfaction, calm them down, and offer a solution to their specific problem.

l. Hyperbolic Discounting: According to this cognitive bias, people tend to prefer smaller, immediate rewards over larger, delayed rewards. This means that immediate gratification is preferred over long-term benefits with higher returns (Hyperbolic Discounting - The Decision Lab, n.d.). This bias is utilised in sales and marketing to capitalise on people's preference for immediate rewards over delayed ones. This effect is achieved by mentioning limited-time offers, 'buy now, pay later,' and free shipping (Hart, M., 2021).

In conclusion, understanding cognitive biases is crucial for salespeople to enhance their effectiveness and foster strong customer relationships. By incorporating cognitive biases, salespeople can tailor their approaches to meet customers' needs and expectations. However, ethical considerations should take precedence when integrating cognitive biases into the sales strategy.

7.6 Reflections:

In my sales journey, I have navigated the market's highs and lows, experiencing the joys and challenges of selling office furniture across various economic conditions. Over the past 32 years, I have experienced the different sales phases.

In the 1990s, Traditional Selling techniques were used to sell office furniture. Business houses relied heavily on salespersons' face-to-face interactions with prospects and customers. Customers or prospects made showroom visits to view and evaluate the furniture on display. Salespersons interacted with prospects and customers, explaining product features and benefits while developing rapport during these transactions.

Salespeople reached prospects through cold calling, direct mail, trade shows, and conferences. Their operations were confined to specific geographical locations, and expanding beyond these boundaries was time-consuming and expensive.

Printed catalogues and brochures provided detailed explanations of the product range, specifications, features, benefits, and prices. Customers placed orders by mail, fax, or phone. Advertisements were primarily displayed through newspapers, magazines, and other media.

In 2000, email was a standard communication tool, facilitating frequent and direct communications with prospects or clients. Businesses established an online presence through professionally designed company websites. Online catalogues replaced printed ones, making it easy for prospects to access them. Products had a better reach.

In 2020, technological advancements revolutionised sales. The COVID-19 pandemic changed the selling scenario. To survive, businesses adopted new methods to reach their customers. They used online selling, e-commerce platforms, Zoom meetings, or video conferencing to interact with customers. Selling through social media became common, breaking geographical boundaries.

Technological advancements will spur innovation in selling methods in the future. Consequently, it becomes imperative for salespeople to upgrade their technical skills to stay aligned with these advancements. However, a salesperson's intrinsic value cannot be replaced. It remains fundamental to their success. Thoughts, Feelings, and Behaviours form the core of a salesperson's intrinsic value, enabling them to build a strong rapport with customers, effectively communicate product features and benefits, provide solutions, and adapt to ever-changing sales scenarios.

Thoughts, Feelings, and Behaviours are linked to the Integrated Adult ego state in Transactional Analysis, which is the core subject of the research work. The Integrated Adult ego state is characterised by rational, objective, and balanced information processing, directly influencing a person's thoughts, feelings, and behaviours. In this ego state, a person's actions are grounded in reality, leading to compelling and harmonious interactions. This can contribute significantly to sales success.

Step into the Next Part... A Wealth of
Knowledge Awaits...

P A R T III:

RESEARCH JOURNEY

Chapter 8

Research Silhouette

The office furniture market has been evolving, making it more complex due to the diversity of designs and changing customer preferences. To maintain long-term productive customer relations, salespersons might need to understand the customers cognitively to explore the mental processes that influence customers' behaviours, decisions, and preferences. Thus, the research objective was to identify the dominant functional ego states of salespeople and the role of the Integrated Adult ego state, as described in Transactional Analysis, in the Cognitive selling of office furniture in the Kingdom of Bahrain.

Well-planned research was designed to draw valid and trustworthy conclusions. It helped collect quality data, use credible resources, and analyse the data to find answers to the study's questions.

This study employed a qualitative research design, which necessitated an understanding of the participants' thoughts, opinions, and experiences.

The interpretivist research philosophy was ideal for this study, "Identifying the Role of the Integrated Adult Ego State in the Cognitive Selling Approach: A Study on Office Furniture in the Kingdom of Bahrain." The study employed qualitative data, including interviews and opinions, to gain in-depth knowledge of human behaviour and subjective experiences. Interpretivism philosophy aims to understand and interpret social phenomena through individuals' subjective experiences and perspectives (*Bridge Research Consulting | Interpretivism Research Philosophy: Unveiling Its Power and Potential*, n.d.).

The population of the present study consists of office furniture salespeople in the Kingdom of Bahrain and experts in the field.

The study used a Purposive sampling or selective sampling method. The sample included successful sales professionals at various career stages, possessing a wealth of experience and expertise in the field. The participants from various nationalities provided sufficient cultural variety for the study. The objective of selecting this diverse group is to enrich the study by offering a holistic understanding of sales dynamics. Two surveys were conducted with the same sample group to find the dominant ego state and cognitive factors.

The study was comprehensive, and expert interviews with Industry and Academic experts willing to share their knowledge and experience facilitated an understanding of current practices, innovations, and theoretical viewpoints. The interviews used semi-structured formats to facilitate in-depth discussions on critical topics.

8.1 Data Collection:

Data collection is the heart of any research study. Data was systematically collected to ensure accuracy and reliability in understanding research problems, enabling insightful interpretations, and making informed decisions.

To make the study more reliable and impactful, the following methods were used for data collection:

Two questionnaires were administered to the same sample to collect reliable and valid data.

1. Questionnaire: The first questionnaire was designed to assess and measure ego states in a systematic and quantifiable manner, thus finding the participants' dominant ego state.

   The second questionnaire was used to identify the factors associated with cognitive selling. It was designed to examine various cognitive factors that contribute to the successful sale of office furniture. A pilot survey was conducted to test the questionnaire on a small sample, ensuring reliability and validity, and identifying potential difficulties in answering the questions. After analysing the results from the pilot survey, confusing questions were corrected. The accuracy of the different elements in the questionnaire was checked. Finally, the questionnaires were easy to understand and answer.

2. Interviewing the experts: Industry and academic experts willing to share their knowledge and experience were interviewed to obtain unique and diverse perspectives not available through other sources. The interviews helped collect detailed information and expert views on the subject. The interviews were natural conversations.

3. Existing literature: Referring to the existing literature helped to extract relevant data or information on the subject under study. It helped me gain in-depth knowledge and understanding of the subject. Existing literature provided evidence and support to strengthen the hypotheses and conclusions.

8.2. Methods of Analysis:

The methods of analysis played a crucial role in the research study. This included the techniques and procedures used to examine and interpret the collected data. It established credibility, explained the data collection and analysis, allowed replication, and linked to the literature.

The methods of analysis used in the study were as follows:

a. The RANK function in Excel was used to find the position of a particular factor under observation. RANK in Excel helped identify the ranks of different factors, such as 1st, 2nd, 3rd, and so on.

b. Aggregate Value Analysis: In data aggregation, raw data was collected, centralised, and aggregated (Recker, 2023). The aggregated data was then analysed to derive meaningful conclusions.

c. Content Analysis: The data collected from the responses was systematically analysed based on the words, themes, and concepts. They were grouped to draw meaningful and credible conclusions.

8.3 Ethical Considerations:

The research considered the following ethical considerations to get valuable and trustworthy responses.

a. Participation in the survey was voluntary, without coercion or pressure. This helped the participants provide honest, accurate, thoughtful responses, resulting in reliable data. Moreover, voluntary participation reduced the bias in responses, as participants' rights were respected.

b. The respondents were informed about the purpose of the survey, which was necessary to determine whether they would participate. This developed trust, motivating participants to give thoughtful and reliable responses.

c. The respondents' privacy was maintained. When the responses were secured, the respondents provided honest, robust, and accurate information.

d. Ensured the survey did not cause harm to the respondents. This built trust in the research process, allowing the participants to feel safe and comfortable in providing honest responses.

e. Honesty and Integrity were maintained to ensure that the data collected was not manipulated or misinterpreted, leading to correct conclusions.

f. The research participants were approached with respect and dignity, treated with fairness and care during the research process.

The above ethical considerations not only protected the rights of the respondents but also enhanced the validity and reliability of the research findings (Academy & Academy, 2023b).

Read On... For More Revelations...

Chapter 9

Observations, Results, Analysis, and Insights

The research was designed to explore the variegated aspects of cognitive selling and Transactional Analysis through a multi-phase approach. The study was divided into three parts, as outlined in the data collection section, to determine the factors affecting cognitive selling and TA.

This chapter enumerates the observations gathered from the research and offers valuable insights on the subject under focus. For the benefit of the readers, the data is presented visually using pie charts and bar charts. This will simplify the complex data and make it easier to understand the critical aspects of our observation.

(Survey 1)
9.1 Portrait of the Participants:

As mentioned earlier, the study used a purposeful sampling of successful and experienced office furniture sales professionals working in Bahrain. Successful sales professionals have effective strategies and techniques that contribute to their success. They bring experience and practical knowledge to discern what works and what does not. Their ideas can be integrated into the sales model to make it unique and compelling.

a. **Age-wise classification:**

The table below illustrates the age-wise classification of the sample.

Age in Years	% of Total	Cumulative %
35-40	25	25
41-50	40	65
51-60	20	85
Above 60	15	100

Table 1: Frequencies of Age

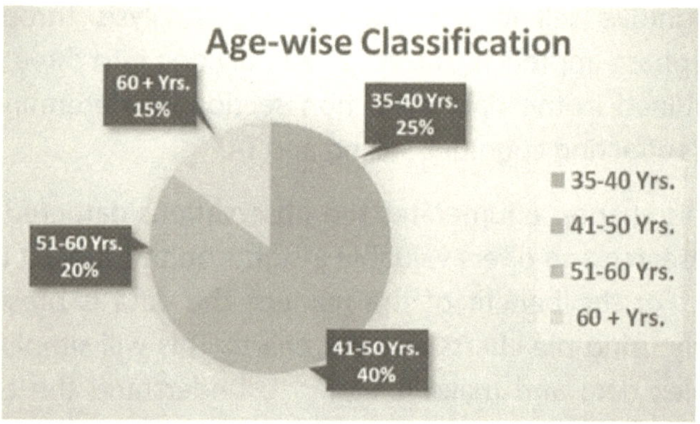

Figure 24: Frequencies of Age

b. **Experience-wise classification:**

The table below illustrates the Experience-wise classification of the sample.

Experience	% of Total	Cumulative %
<10 yrs.	20	20
10-15 yrs.	15	35
16-20 yrs.	25	60
> 20 yrs.	40	100

Table 2: Frequencies of Experience

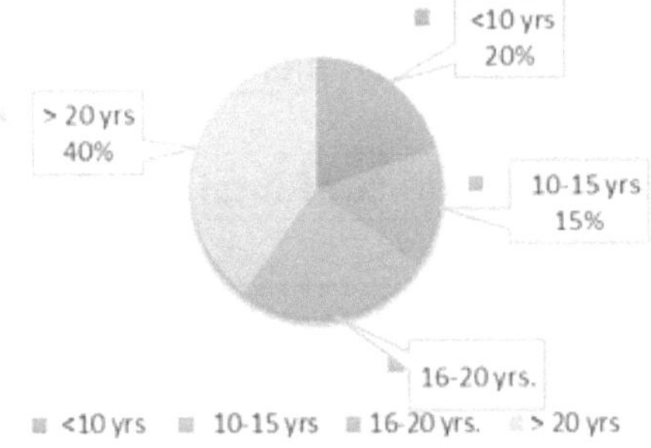

Figure 25: Frequencies of Experience

c. **Education-wise classification:**

The table below illustrates the Education-wise classification of the sample.

Education	% of Total	Cumulative %
Undergraduate	0	0
Graduate	65	65
Postgraduate	35	100

Table 3: Frequencies of Education-wise Classification

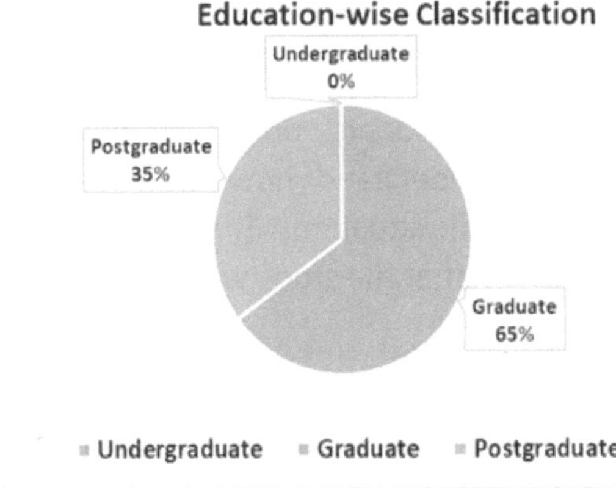

Figure 26: Frequencies of Educational Qualifications

d. **Designation-wise classification:**

The table below illustrates the Designation-wise classification of the sample.

Designation	% of Total	Cumulative %
Sales Executive	25	25
Sales Manager	30	55
Sr. Sales Manager	45	100

Table 4: Frequencies of Designations

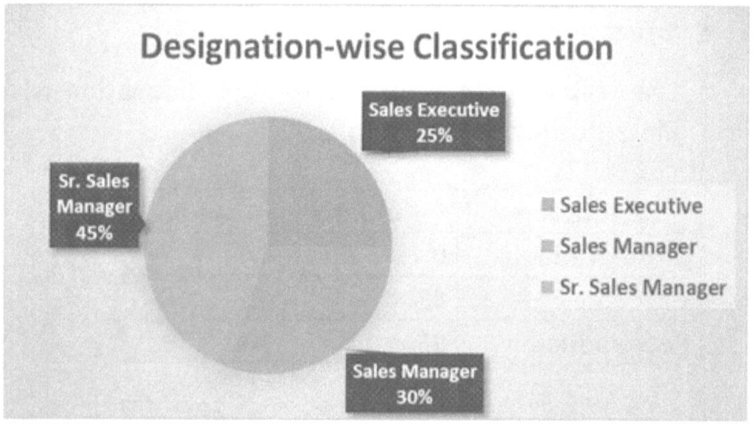

Figure 27: Frequencies of Designations

e. **Dominant Ego States of Participants:**

Identifying respondents' dominant ego states was necessary to understand how they feel, think, and behave in specific situations. This would be a valuable indicator of whether the study was on the right track.

A well-structured questionnaire was distributed among a diverse group of sales professionals. The questionnaire was designed to reveal the dominant ego states based on established psychological factors.

The collected data was categorised and calculated into Controlling Parent, Nurturing Parent, Functional Adult, Natural Child, and Adapted Child. The collected data is presented below:

Dominant Ego States	Percentage of Respondents
Functional Adult	40
Nurturing Parent	30
Controlling Parent	15
Natural Child	5
Adapted Child	10
Total	100

Table 5: Summary of Dominant Ego States.

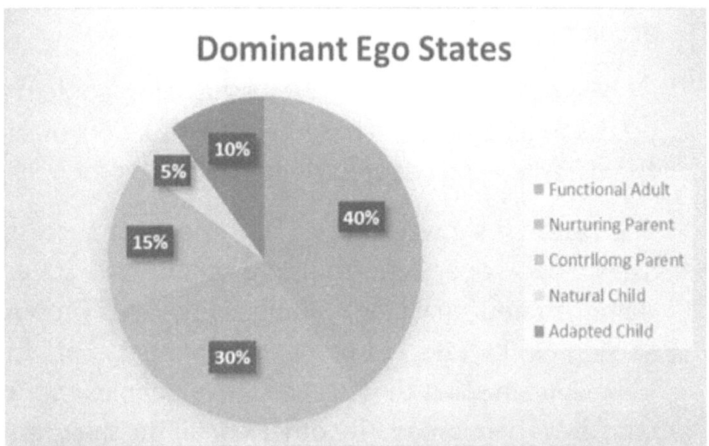

Figure 28: Dominant Ego States

The above observations lead to the following conclusions:

Dominant Ego States:

1. The Egogram revealed that all participants (Salespersons) had access to all five ego states - Controlling Parent, Nurturing Parent, Functional Adult, Natural Child, and

Adopted Child. This demonstrated that they could utilise the full range of thoughts, feelings, and behaviours associated with each of the ego states. They could operate from the appropriate ego state as the situation demanded. This would enable salespersons to interact freely and allow customers to express their thoughts and concerns. This would help them understand the customer's psychology, which is crucial for effective cognitive selling.

There was 'no exclusion' of any ego state. For the respondents, no ego state was closed. So, salespersons were able to respond effectively to customers in different situations. They could understand how their customers perceived them and adjust their actions accordingly.

We can conclude that successful salespeople have access to all ego states based on the situation, making them flexible and adaptable when tackling problems.

2. The research showed that 40% of the most successful salespeople operated from the Adult ego state. It demonstrated that logic, objectivity, and problem-solving skills are essential components of their behaviour. In sales, the most effective people are those who are fact-oriented. The other side of the salesperson was also covered, who employed logical thinking and straightforward communication to accomplish the tasks. When they faced the challenges, they were practical and realistic.

3. The 30% segment with the Nurturing Parent ego state consisted of salespeople who demonstrated empathy, the ability to give their customers hope and, with their help, facilitated the sale. Salespeople who employed

this type of communication established deep connections with their clients by providing tailored advice and creating a supportive, safe, and emotionally comfortable environment for both parties.

4. Experienced and successful salespeople operate more frequently from Adult and Nurturing Parent ego states. The reason might be that through experience, they developed logical ability, objective decision-making, self-awareness, and emotional intelligence, resulting in strong customer relations.

It can be concluded that most respondents had Functional Adult and Nurturing Parent ego states. Fewer respondents had the Controlling Parent and Adapted Child states, and very few had the Natural Child ego state. Thus, the group under study exhibited more mature and nurturing behaviours.

Egogram reveals the communication style of the people under study. Understanding ego states enables salespeople to enhance their communication and foster effective customer rapport. Salespersons can better understand the dynamics of interactions and respond more effectively and appropriately, thereby enhancing the cognitive selling approach.

Designation Pattern:

The distribution of designations in this study illuminates several interesting points about the role of the Integrated Adult ego state in cognitive selling.

45% of the respondents were Senior Sales Managers. It was suggested that individuals with more experience and higher positions are likelier to have a well-developed adult ego state. This state of mind, characterised by clear thinking, unbiased perspectives, and thoughtful consideration of emotions, is crucial for selling thoughtfully.

The presence of Sales Executives (25%) and Sales Managers (30%) also indicated that the development of the Adult ego state was not restricted to the most senior positions. This suggests a growth process where salespersons at various career stages can contribute to selling, leveraging a range of experiences and levels of self-awareness.

The distribution shows a balanced representation across different levels of sales positions. This balance is crucial for understanding how the Integrated Adult ego state impacts cognitive selling across various career stages.

Ultimately, the observations reveal how salespeople at various levels utilise their ego states to sell effectively. It demonstrates why ongoing professional growth is essential throughout a sales career.

Adding a different dimension to this observation, we could infer that training programmes aimed at developing the Integrated Adult ego state to support cognitive selling should be tailored to the career stages of sales professionals. This ensures that each group benefits from the training, tailored to their current role and experience level.

Educational Stratification:

The distribution of academic education in this study furnishes us with fascinating insights into the role of the Integrated Adult ego state in cognitive selling:

1. In the sample of successful salespersons, 65% were graduates, and 35% were postgraduates. This suggested that higher educational levels allowed salespersons to operate from an Adult ego state. In the process of getting higher education, salespeople develop the skills of critical thinking, problem-solving, and emotional intelligence, all of which are key components of the Integrated Adult ego state.

2. The absence of undergraduate respondents implies that those with only an undergraduate education may not yet have developed the Adult ego state to a level deemed effective for cognitive selling. Therefore, office furniture companies often avoided hiring undergraduates for sales jobs because these roles require specific skills.

3. The high number of graduates and postgraduates showed that this level of schooling involved targeted training, research, and hands-on experiences. These factors helped to boost the overall growth of salespeople.

The diversity of academic backgrounds underscores the pivotal role of ongoing learning and career growth. These factors are instrumental in cultivating the Integrated Adult ego state, a prerequisite for effective cognitive selling. This insight can inspire and guide hiring choices and the development of training programmes.

Age Spectrum Insights:

The survey found that 65% of successful salespeople were between 35 and 50 years old. This suggested that most of them had a mix of experience and knowledge, which was important for effective selling.

Among these, 40% were aged 41 to 50. At this stage, they likely honed their selling skills through years of practice and learning, instilling confidence and reassurance in their decision-making abilities.

The survey included both younger and older age groups to gather a diverse range of experiences and viewpoints. This helped us gain valuable and positive insights into how the Integrated Adult ego state influences cognitive selling.

Distribution of Experience:

The classification appreciably reflects the variability of tenure among the sample. The most significant proportion (40%) comprised salespersons with more than twenty years of experience, which implied that experienced salespeople could contribute to the study.

Twenty-five percent of the sample had experience between sixteen and twenty years. This category could provide new insights into how mid-career professionals viewed this new perspective towards selling.

The sample consisted of 15% salespeople with ten to fifteen years of experience. This group consisted of middle professionals with knowledge of sales strategies and practices.

Twenty percent of salespeople had less than ten years of experience. This relatively young segment made significant contributions to our studies on cognitive selling.

The sample represented a diverse range of years of service. This could incorporate the opinions and suggestions of a broad spectrum of salespersons in our study.

From the above observations, we can infer that Experience, Education, and Age help a salesperson operate from the Adult ego state. We can explore the reasons behind it.

As salespeople gain more experience, they are exposed to a variety of situations, thereby enhancing their ability to make informed decisions. They learn to differentiate between right and wrong in a given situation, enabling them to make logical and objective decisions. Their decisions are based on information rather than assumptions or feelings, reflecting their mature approach to decision-making.

As salespeople age, they tend to become more emotionally mature, resulting in a more thoughtful and rational approach to handling situations. They have a better perspective on the world and make multiple objective conclusions.

Education is crucial in providing salespersons with the necessary information and knowledge to make informed choices. Higher education fosters critical thinking and analytical skills, essential for effective decision-making in the sales industry.

Thus, integrating experience, age, and education enables salespeople to operate from the Adult ego state, which involves logical and informed decision-making.

9.2 Observations, Results, Analysis, and Insights (Survey 2):

Furthermore, the research's second part focused on the specifics of cognitive selling. The same sample was approached with another set of questionnaires to determine the various factors and their importance in Cognitive selling.

9.2.1. Research on Components of Cognitive Selling:

In this study, the components of cognitive selling were identified, and participants were asked to rank the importance of these components. The study included the following six components of cognitive selling originating from the Parent, Adult, and Child ego states.

1. Listening to customers' concerns: Active listening is a crucial aspect of Cognitive selling. To facilitate a sale, the salesperson must understand the customer's needs

and respond accordingly. Listening to customers helps build trust, identify needs, tailor solutions, overcome objections, and enhance communication, among other benefits. When a salesperson listens to customers' concerns, they operate from the Nurturing Parent ego state as it involves support, empathy, and reassurance to the customer.

2. Helping Customers Make Decisions: This component of cognitive selling enables salespeople to deliver top-quality customer service and maintain strong relationships with clients. In this case, the salesperson helps the customer make the right choice, saving them time and energy. A salesperson utilises the Nurturing Parent ego state in this situation to help customers make informed decisions. This ego state is characterised by caring, supportive, and guiding behaviour. Moreover, the salesperson provides emotional support and assurance in such situations.

3. Gathering information about customers' needs and preferences is the basis of cognitive selling. This information is crucial in determining customer preferences and providing the most effective recommendations. A salesperson operates from an Adult ego state while collecting information about customers' needs and preferences, requiring objective analysis, critical thinking, and logical processing.

4. Explaining Product Features and Benefits: This component of cognitive selling enables salespeople to explain product features and benefits to customers effectively. The customer evaluates the pros and cons of the product to make an informed decision. A salesperson typically operates from the adult ego state,

which involves logical thinking, objective analysis, and solution-focused communication.

5. Humour and friendliness: This component of cognitive selling utilises humour and friendliness to create a positive impression and establish a rapport with customers, making them feel like friends of the salesperson. This creates a lasting impression on customers. Free Child ego state is used, which is characterised by emotional expressions, playfulness, and spontaneity.

6. Enthusiastic and Energetic: This component of cognitive selling is impactful. A salesperson who is Enthusiastic and Energetic stands out and draws customers' attention. Here, the salesperson operates from a Free Child ego state, which involves genuine emotional expression, excitement, and spontaneity.

The table mentions the "ranks" of the components for cognitive selling. This illustrates the prioritisation of various elements within the cognitive selling process, which are closely aligned with the conversational factors essential for successful selling.

Components of Cognitive Selling	Rank
Listening to Customers' concerns	1 (Most Important)
Gathering info about customers' needs & preferences	2 (Very Important)
Explaining Product Features & Benefits	3 (Important)
Helping Customers make decisions	4 (Fairly Important)
Enthusiastic & Energetic	5 (Moderately Important)
Humour and Friendliness	6 (Somewhat Important)

Table 6: Ranks of Components of Cognitive Selling

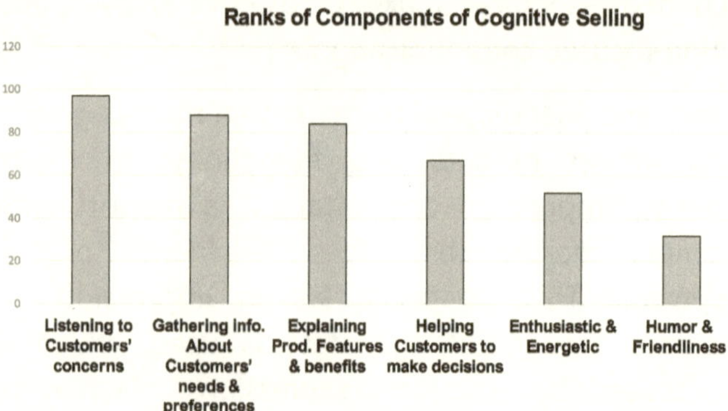

Figure 29: Ranks of Components of Cognitive Selling

The following insights stem from the above observations:

1. **Listening to Customers' Concerns:**

   The survey clearly shows that "listening to customers' concerns" was ranked first in terms of importance. This means that this factor is important in cognitive selling for the following reasons:

   a. Building Trust and Rapport: Customers have confidence in salespersons who take the time to address their issues because they recognise that their voices have been heard. In weaving relationships, trust is vital to foster a long-term relationship with them. This helps to repeat business.

   b. Needs identification: Paying close attention to the customer can help the salesperson gain a deeper understanding of the customer's wants, needs, and concerns. This enables salespersons to tailor their service by offering solutions to customers' problems.

   c. Solutions to Problems: When working with customers, salespeople can find the root cause of their problems. If the resources are available, the issues can be addressed.

Cognitive selling involves listening to understand customers, which should be a top priority. Listening to customers' concerns becomes a building block of cognitive selling.

2. **Gathering Information About Customers' Needs and Preferences:**

The survey ranked this factor second in importance. The high ranking highlights the significance of the salesperson's efforts to delve into the details of the customers and adjust their approach for better results. The customers' requirements and interests are instrumental in suggesting appropriate solutions. This highlights the importance of customised communications in the selling cycle.

When a salesperson shows interest in exploring the customers' requirements, a sense of trust prevails in their relationship. This trust leads to healthy relationships.

Satisfying customers' specific requirements to make them happy is a good selling tactic. A satisfied customer will be an asset to the organisation, as they will make repeat purchases and become valuable referrals.

Data on customers is important from a strategic perspective, as it provides insight into changing patterns and trends. This information is crucial for developing effective sales strategies, designing products, and implementing promotional efforts that benefit both customers and the organisation.

Thus, by gathering information about the customer's needs, salespersons generate a more direct and empathetic sales dialogue that strengthens cognitive selling.

3. Explaining Product Features & Benefits:

This component was ranked third in the order of importance. It highlights the importance of clearly conveying the features and benefits of products to customers. It also highlights the importance of clear, concise, and informative communication about the product and its suitability for customers. This will help customers make informed purchasing decisions, as they can understand the competitive advantages of products over others. Clear communication facilitates higher sales conversions. Transparent communication fosters trust between the salesperson and the customer, leading to repeat business.

4. Helping Customers Make Decisions:

The fact that this component was ranked fourth indicated that the above three are more important in cognitive selling. However, helping customers make decisions is still important in cognitive selling. It creates a sense of support and trust as the salesperson helps to reduce the mental effort required by the customer to make the right decision. When customers feel guided and supported, they tend to reciprocate and are more likely to make a purchase.

5. Enthusiastic and Energetic Nature of a Salesperson:

As mentioned earlier, the fifth position of this factor indicates the presence of other prioritised factors in cognitive selling. This component is also important in selling. Salespersons' enthusiasm and energy level can set a positive tone in sales interactions. A salesperson's enthusiasm can capture the customer's attention and interest, showcasing their enthusiasm.

Some customers may perceive excessive enthusiasm as pushy, which can make them feel pressured to make a purchase. In some cases, customers doubted the salesperson's intentions. However, salespeople must strike a balance between their enthusiasm and professionalism, while also understanding the customer's needs and expectations.

6. **Humour and Friendliness:**

In the survey, Humour and Friendliness were ranked last. We can assign several reasons for this. Customers may prefer a more straightforward and professional approach to purchasing office furniture. Office furniture customers may associate humour and friendliness with a lack of professionalism and prefer a more knowledgeable and serious approach.

The type of products sold may influence customers' perceptions of salespeople. When products are technical or highly valued, customers may prioritise salespersons' expertise and knowledge over their sense of humour and friendliness. Thus, each product has unique selling demands, and salespeople adapt their cognitive strategies accordingly to achieve success.

9.2.2. Research on "Cognitive Factors Influencing Customers' Purchase Decisions.":

Customers tend to have complex thought processes when they make decisions. It is necessary to investigate the cognitive factors that determine their choices. These cognitive factors include the mental processes that shape customer perceptions, evaluations, and decisions. These thought processes are responsible for their behaviour and ultimately influence the decision to make a purchase. An understanding of these cognitive factors informs a practical sales approach, enabling better targeting of the target customers.

The study identified twelve cognitive factors that affect customers' decisions to purchase a product. Respondents were asked to indicate whether they considered each cognitive factor important by marking "YES." The factors under consideration are presented below:

1. **Salesperson's ability to identify the customer's requirements:**

   When a salesperson identifies the customer's specific wants or needs, he or she can find resources to fulfil those requirements, satisfying the customer. This personalised interaction can impact the customer's decision, favouring the salesperson.

2. **Salesperson's empathy and understanding of the customer's situation:**

   A salesperson's empathy and understanding build trust, reduce cognitive dissonance, and enable a strong emotional connection. This can influence the customer's perception of the product or service, increasing their likelihood of making a purchase.

3. **Presenting the product as a solution to the customer's challenges:**

   Customers look for solutions to their problems. When a customer sees the product as a direct answer to their specific needs, the product becomes indispensable to them and thus influences their buying decision.

4. **Salesman's product knowledge and expertise in problem-solving:**

When a salesperson possesses in-depth product knowledge and experience in problem-solving, it fosters confidence in the products, and customers trust their recommendations. A salesperson's expertise can reduce the customer's uncertainty about the products and make them feel secure in their buying decisions.

5. **Product demonstration before selling:**

The Product demonstration amounts to "seeing is believing." It allows customers to see the products perform live. It can reinforce the brand's credibility. Demonstrations can create an instinct to buy.

6. **The salesman's ability to effectively handle objections and questions:**

The ability to address objections confidently makes a salesperson more credible. When objections are handled effectively, the risk factor influencing the buying process is reduced.

7. **Salesperson's respect, honesty, and transparency in communication:**

The customer feels valued in respectful interactions. Honesty leads to trust. Transparent communications reduce cognitive dissonance. The above factors foster long-term customer relationships, leading to repeat purchases.

8. **Social Media presence**:

   Social media validation presence influences customer decision-making as it can create a sense of trust and credibility. Frequent exposure keeps the brand at the forefront of potential customers' minds, allowing them to see real-time feedback on the brand.

9. **Salesperson's ability to close the sale at mutually agreeable terms and conditions:**

   When the terms and conditions are mutually agreeable, customers perceive the deal as fair and balanced, resulting in increased customer satisfaction. Transparent terms build customer confidence, leading to their commitment to make a purchase.

10. **The concept of "the higher the price, the better the product."**

    Often, the high price of products is associated with better quality, better performance, higher social status, brand exclusivity, and luxury. This is known as the price-quality heuristic, which influences customer decision-making.

11. **The company's reputation:**

    Customers tend to believe that reputable companies offer quality and reliable products and therefore, perceive less risk in dealing with them. Reputation can even influence potential customers' decisions.

12. **Brand Image:**

    The brand image helps a product stand out. It can foster an emotional connection, loyalty, quality assurance, and trust, ultimately leading to repeat purchases.

The survey results revealed the following percentages of respondents who answered "yes" to various cognitive factors influencing purchase decisions:

Cognitive Factors Influencing Customers' Purchase Decisions	Percentage
1. Salesperson's Ability to identify the customer's requirements.	100
2. The salesperson's ability to close the sale at a mutually agreeable Terms and conditions.	90
3. Presenting the product as a solution to the customer's challenges.	85
4. Salesperson's product knowledge and expertise in problem-solving.	85
5. Salesperson's respect, honesty, and transparency in communication.	80
6. The salesperson's ability to effectively handle objections and questions.	80
7. Salesperson's empathy and understanding of the customer's situation.	75
8. Product demonstration before selling.	55
9. Social Media presence.	55
10. The company's reputation.	50
11. Brand image	45
12. The concept of "the higher the price, the better the product."	15

Table 7: Cognitive Factors Influencing Customers' Purchase Decisions

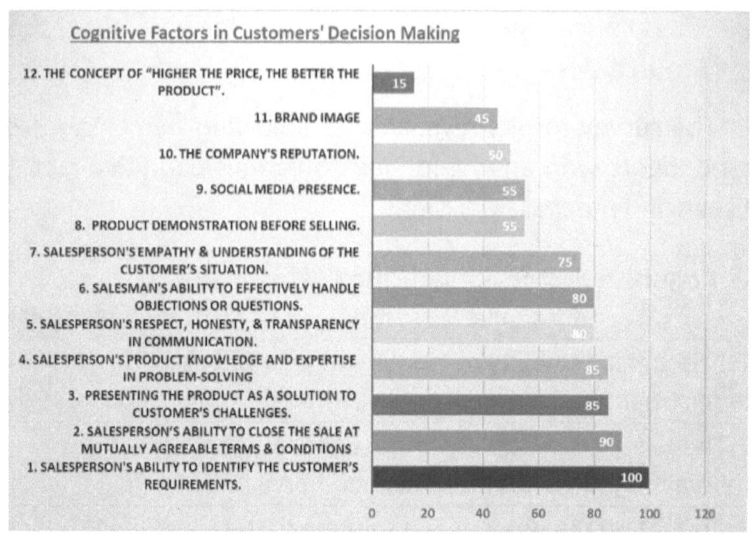

Figure 30: Cognitive Factors in Customers' Decision-Making

Based on the above observations, I could derive the following insights on Cognitive Factors Influencing Customers' Purchase Decisions:

In Cognitive selling, understanding the cognitive factors—often the mental processes that influence customers' thoughts, feelings, and behaviour—is crucial. These factors influence customers' purchase decisions. The survey results are listed above in descending order of importance—Sr. No. 1 is the Most Important, and Sr. No. 12 is the least important.

1. Salesperson's Ability to Identify the Customer's Requirements: This is the cornerstone of cognitive selling. A sales approach cannot be crafted unless the salesperson understands the customer's needs and requirements. This helps the salesperson tailor the products and services to each customer, making them more appealing and relevant. The cognitive abilities involved are Active Listening, Empathy, Critical

Thinking, Problem Solving, Attention to detail, Memory, and Questioning Skills.

2. Salesperson's ability to close the sale at mutually agreeable terms and conditions. This was ranked second in the survey. In cognitive selling, mutual agreement in closing sales is considered highly important. This ensures the benefit of customers and salespersons. It promotes trust, satisfaction, and value. This highlights the importance of building trust and relationships, ensuring customer satisfaction, fairness, maximising value, and overall customer experience.

   This requires negotiation and communication skills, in addition to other cognitive skills.

3. Presenting the product as a solution to customers' challenges ranked third. This underscores the role of solution-based selling in today's market. It indicates the shift from traditional selling to solution-focused selling. This helps salespeople create more meaningful and impactful interactions with customers. Product benefits will be more appealing to customers, justifying their purchase.

   In addition to other cognitive skills, this factor requires critical thinking, problem-solving, logical reasoning, and adaptability.

4. Salesperson's product knowledge and expertise in problem-solving. This was also ranked third and showed that customers valued the salesperson who knew the product well and explained how it met their specific needs—the salesperson's ability to solve problems added value to the customer's experience.

The cognitive skills required in this case are Analytical Thinking, Learning Agility, Memory, Research Skills, Diagnostic Skills, and a Continuous Improvement Mindset.

5. Salespersons' respect, honesty, and transparency while communicating were ranked fourth. These attributes were important to customers, though other considerations were of greater emphasis. Respect, honesty, and transparency are at the core of trust in any relationship, and support is needed to establish a genuine connection with the customers. These qualities should be unified with others in a successful sale.

    Cognitive skills required are Empathy, Self-Regulation, Social Awareness, Active Listening, and Effective Communication.

6. The salesperson's ability to effectively handle objections and questions. The fourth rank revealed that these factors were significant in cognitive selling, as they had a substantial influence on the customer's decision. This skill is crucial in building trust, clarifying concepts, advancing understanding, and facilitating informed decision-making.

    The cognitive skills required are Active Listening, Critical Thinking, Adaptability, Problem Solving, Memory Recall and Persuasion.

7. The salesperson's empathy and understanding of the customer's situation. The fifth-place ranking implied that cognitive selling values "empathy and understanding of the customer's situation," but it might not be the paramount concern for customers. Customers might consider other factors, such

as identifying customers' requirements, product knowledge, and problem-solving skills, to have a more significant impact on sales transactions.

The cognitive skills required to develop empathy and understand customer situations are Active Listening (to gather crucial information about customer requirements), Emotional Intelligence (to manage emotions), Perspective Taking (to see things from the customer's viewpoint), Critical Thinking (to make a reasoned judgement), Memory Recall (to remember customer interactions over a while), and Cultural Awareness (to understand the customer's cultural background).

8. Product demonstration before selling. This was ranked sixth. Product demonstrations enhance the customer's overall product experience, appealing to both their senses and cognitive abilities. Though this factor is important, other factors also play a significant role in decision-making.

   The cognitive skills required to persuade prospects through product demonstration are Product Knowledge (to demonstrate the product values), Communication Skills (to clarify customers' doubts), Visualisation (to visualise product benefits), Persuasion (to influence buyers' decisions), Storytelling (to illustrate the product's value and impact), and confidence (to influence buyers' confidence in purchase decisions).

9. Social Media presence. This was also ranked sixth. This indicates that other cognitive factors have a significant influence on customers' decision-making. Although social media plays a role in creating brand awareness

and emotional connection, customers consider direct interactions, tailored solutions, and problem-solving skills to be important when purchasing office furniture.

The cognitive skills associated with social media presence are creativity, communication skills, networking, strategic planning, and content creation.

10. The company's reputation: This was ranked seventh. A company's reputation can influence cognitive selling by affecting buyers' perceptions, trust, and overall reliability. This ranking suggests that though company reputation is an influential factor, customers prioritise direct interaction with salespersons, problem-solving abilities, and tailored solutions.

    The cognitive skills required to build a strong company reputation are strategic thinking, visualisation, analytical thinking, ethical judgement, and networking skills.

11. Brand image: This was ranked eighth, as brand image plays a crucial role in cognitive selling by providing trust and reliability, emotional connection, differentiation, consistency, and fostering customer loyalty. This indicates that customers value other cognitive skills, such as direct interaction, problem-solving abilities, product knowledge, and persuasive techniques.

    Creating a brand image requires several cognitive skills to differentiate the brand from others. Some skills involved are creativity, visualisation, communication skills, analytical thinking, ethical judgement, and networking.

12. The concept of "the higher the price, the better the product" was ranked ninth. This suggests that the notion "the higher the price, the better the product"

is not always accurate. In a few cases, higher-priced products are viewed as status symbols, perceived as of higher quality, and associated with a stronger brand image. However, purchasers of office furniture look for value for money. They are price-sensitive and prioritise features and performance over price.

This concept relies on the customer's cognitive process of associating quality with price. Marketing professionals utilise communication skills, persuasion techniques, strategic thinking, visualisation, and brand management to shape and influence this perception.

In Cognitive Selling, understanding the importance of cognitive factors influencing purchase decisions is crucial. This enables businesses to formulate sales strategies that align with customer needs, ultimately leading to increased sales success.

9.2.3. Research on "Salesperson's Characteristics that Attract Customers.":

It is pretty natural for customers to prefer dealing with salespeople they like. They feel more comfortable discussing their requirements, leading to honest interactions. The interaction becomes pleasant, resulting in a positive buying experience that leads to repeat purchases.

To succeed in sales, salespeople must win over their customers. This study has identified and ranked the key traits of salespeople who possess these skills.

Product Knowledge: Customers trust salespeople who thoroughly understand the products they sell. A salesperson with extensive product knowledge can educate customers on the product's features, benefits, and usage. This helps salespeople create a positive impression, allowing customers to like and trust them.

Communication Skills: Effective communication skills involve active listening. This allows the salesperson to understand and tailor the customer's needs and preferences. The customers will feel valued and understood. Pleasant and engaging interactions leave a lasting impression.

Concern for Customers' Interest: When a customer realises that a salesperson is genuinely concerned with their benefits and not focused solely on selling and making money, trust is established. Customers are more likely to be loyal to such a salesperson. They tilt their balance towards a salesperson who patiently understands their needs and offers solutions to their satisfaction.

Reliability and trustworthiness of salespeople: When customers perceive salespeople as reliable and trustworthy, they are more likely to be drawn to them. They feel they can depend on such salespeople and foster long-term business relationships.

Empathy: An empathetic salesperson establishes an emotional connection with customers. They see things from the customers' perspectives and act to make them comfortable and respected. The customer feels heard, valued, and understood. Customers will surely like such salespersons.

Patience: Patience is important for a salesperson. A patient salesperson can remain calm, listen carefully to the customer's needs and preferences, and understand what the customer is looking for. They peacefully handle complaints and objections. Customers prefer to interact with patient salespeople. This creates a more positive and relaxed customer experience. Customers feel more satisfied and become more loyal.

Confidence: Salespeople who exude self-assurance make customers feel they can rely on and trust them. They remain calm and collected in the face of challenging situations. They demonstrate faith in their company and the products they sell, which helps create a positive customer experience. They build up trust and credibility, which are crucial to selling.

The table below highlights the important factors customers consider when evaluating a salesperson. The ranks indicate the level of importance of each factor. The survey results are presented below:

Salesperson's Characteristics that Attract Customers	Total	Rank
Product knowledge/problem-solving skills	89	1
Communication skills	85	2
Reliability/Trustworthiness of salespersons	82	3
Concern for customers' interest	80	4
Empathy	68	5
Patience	67	6
Confidence	64	7

Table 8: Salesperson's Characteristics that Attract Customers

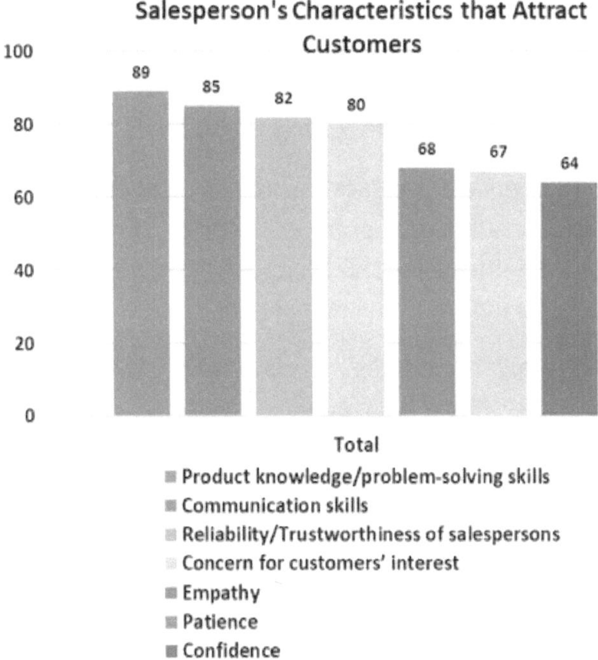

Figure 31: Salesperson's Characteristics that Attract Customers

The insights enumerated below on "Salesperson's Characteristics that Attract Customers" are based on the above observations:

Salespersons' characteristics become a strong base for Cognitive Selling. These characteristics help salespersons attract and retain customers who like to deal with the salespersons they like. Salespersons can gain a competitive advantage by identifying and leveraging these characteristics to foster stronger customer relationships.

The results of the survey showing the ranking of salespersons' characteristics that attract customers are described below:

1. Product knowledge and problem-solving skills: This particular characteristic of the salesperson topped the list. This highlights that customers value salespeople who possess in-depth product knowledge and practical problem-solving skills. Such salespersons provide accurate information, clarify customer doubts, and recommend suitable solutions. Even customers feel confident in their purchase decisions as they deal with salespersons who are experts in their field.

   This sends a message to sales professionals that they should continuously enhance their product knowledge and problem-solving skills to meet customer expectations and foster long-term relationships.

2. Communication skills: This skill ranked second, indicating that it is of great importance in salesperson traits. Salespersons use this skill to make sales transactions more engaging and persuasive. They pay attention to both verbal communication and body language to better understand customer issues.

   This sends a clear message to all salespeople to improve their communication abilities. Successfully communicating one's ideas is what sets them apart from the rest.

3. Reliability/Trustworthiness of Salespersons: The third rank of this characteristic indicates that customers prefer to deal with trustworthy and dependable salespersons. Relationships survive on trust. When customers perceive a salesperson as reliable and trustworthy, they tend to remain loyal to that individual.

   This suggests that sales professionals who fulfil their promises, uphold ethical standards, maintain transparency, and provide accurate information can build long-lasting customer relationships.

4. Concern for customers' interest: This was ranked fourth. This brings out the importance of empathy in sales. Customers like empathetic salespersons who prioritise their interests and benefits. The emphasis is on a customer-centric sales approach.

   We can infer that sales professionals should understand customers' perspectives and offer satisfying solutions that create value for them. This will foster loyalty and encourage repeat purchases.

5. Empathy: This was ranked fifth. Other characteristics, such as product knowledge, problem-solving skills, communication skills, and reliability, may have a more direct impact on sales interactions. Although empathy is ranked fifth, it plays a crucial role in fostering communication and trustworthiness, ultimately contributing to a positive customer experience.

   An empathetic salesperson will approach their customers personally, connecting with them on a deeper level and creating a holistic customer experience.

6. Patience: This was ranked sixth. The primary reason may be that customers placed greater importance on readily displayed skills, such as product knowledge, problem-solving, and communication. A salesperson's patience goes unnoticed in many cases. Such salespersons can remain calm and composed in stressful situations, establish a trusting relationship with customers, and mitigate the overall stress of the sales process.

   Patient salespersons are relationship builders. When dealing with customers, they are patient. They pay attention and obtain data to offer appropriate responses to customer issues. Thus, all these can lead to increased customer satisfaction.

7. Confidence: This was ranked seventh. Confidence is a trait that complements key characteristics such as product knowledge, problem-solving skills, and effective communication. For this reason, it was ranked seventh. Confidence enables salespeople to communicate effectively, handle objections easily, maintain customer comfort, and make informed decisions with confidence.

For salespersons, confidence is a crucial trait as it enhances and complements all other characteristics, making them more effective.

Readers may question why the "professional attire and demeanour of a salesperson" was not included in the research study. Of course, a well-dressed salesperson can create a positive impact on customers. The main reasons why this factor was not included in the study were as follows:

1. The study aimed at the ego states, how salespersons think, feel, and behave, and their influence on cognitive selling.

2. The focus was on psychological factors, such as decision-making, problem-solving, and communication skills, rather than on external appearance.

3. Including professional attire and demeanour would have complicated the study, making it harder to manage.

4. It was assumed that the importance of attire and presentation was widely understood.

As we know, attire and presentation can create a first impression on customers. Some organisations use uniforms to establish an identity and create a brand image. Customers feel comfortable and assured when dealing with such salespersons.

In cognitive selling, the salesperson's characteristics play a crucial role in facilitating fruitful customer interactions, which in turn helps attract and retain customers.

9.3 Experts' Reflections on Integrated Adult Ego in Cognitive Selling:

I have incorporated the comprehensive views of experts to gain a broader perspective on the subject. The primary purpose is to benefit from the experts' wealth of knowledge and experience, thereby gaining a deeper understanding of the subject. This information may not be available from standard sources.

When we discuss cognition, we refer to a higher brain function. It encompasses a range of functions, including Perception, Attention, Learning, Memory, Imagination, Visualisation, Reasoning, Decision-Making, Language, and Problem-Solving. Ideally, a salesperson should have the above mental abilities for successful selling.

In cognitive selling, we should consider the Cognitive abilities of salespersons and customers. Some of the cognitive abilities that salespersons should focus on include communication skills, which enable them to convey their message in a way that the customer can understand. The language should be clear, and paralinguistic factors and body language should be understood. Sales occur when the customer's needs are clearly understood, and solutions are offered to meet the needs. This requires the capacity to think analytically and creatively. Salespersons should possess a high Emotional Quotient (EQ) so that they can effectively understand and manage their own emotions, as well as those of their customers. This is particularly important when dealing with angry or demanding customers. Emotional intelligence is essential for cultivating long-lasting relationships with customers. Customers are not exact. In such cases, salespersons should be able to adapt to different situations.

Understanding the cognitive abilities of customers is important. Salespersons meet customers of different intellectual and emotional levels. Customers employ various decision-making methods, ranging from logical reasoning to emotional and societal factors. The capacity to understand differs. Hence, how the customer understands the salesperson's message is important. Similarly, customers' ability to recall product details varies. In such cases, the salesperson should provide clear and memorable information so that it remains in their memory for a long time. Cognitive biases often influence customers, and the perceived value of the product can change. Recognising these biases will enable salespersons to address potential objections and effectively highlight key benefits.

By considering these cognitive factors, salespeople can create a more personalised and practical selling experience, ultimately leading to better outcomes for both the salesperson and the customer.

The integrated Adult ego state can support the process of cognitive selling. The Integrated Adult ego state is a "colourful" ego state and is considered a fully developed one. This is a single manifestation of Parent, Adult, and Child ego states. In this ego state, a person operates from the rational and logical part of the Adult Ego state, while also integrating the positive elements from the Parent and Child ego states. The person becomes autonomous and functions intellectually, emotionally, and value-based. This ego state enables a salesperson to analyse information and make rational, informed decisions, adhering to their value systems. This results in sales strategies tailored to customers' needs and feedback.

We explore the way the Integrated Adult ego state serves as a support in Cognitive selling:

1. Cognitive selling focuses on addressing clients' needs, underlying thought processes, and challenges. In the Integrated Adult ego state, problem-solving skills are enhanced through the application of logic, facts, and data related to a subject.

2. Cognitive selling demands clear and concise communication. An Integrated Adult ego helps convey information effectively, resulting in better relationships.

3. Integrated Adult ego empowers the clients to deal with their cognitive biases, especially when the information is presented logically and objectively.

4. When dealing with clients in Cognitive selling, there is a need for a strategy change based on customer requirements. Integrated Adult allows flexibility and brings change based on logic.

5. Rational thinking, under the Integrated Adult ego, enables the salesperson to remain emotionally intense in challenging situations, which is excellent for sales.

6. Arguments presented using the Integrated Adult ego state become much more rational, well-thought-out, and consistent. This fosters trust and long-lasting relationships, a core component of Cognitive selling that ensures repeat purchases from clients.

From the above, it is evident that a salesperson can improve their effectiveness in cognitive selling by operating from their Integrated Adult ego state. This is mainly because the Integrated Adult ego state promotes objective decision-making, effective communication, problem-solving skills, emotional management, relationship-building, and objection handling. Salespeople may not possess this skill, but it can be developed through training and practice. The challenges in selling can be overcome by adopting a cognitive selling approach supported by the Integrated Adult ego state.

Let us determine how the above research results can be incorporated into the UniK Psycho-Sales Model.

Continue Reading... To Explore the Model...

PART IV:

UNIK PSYCHO-SALES MODEL

Chapter 10

The Blueprint

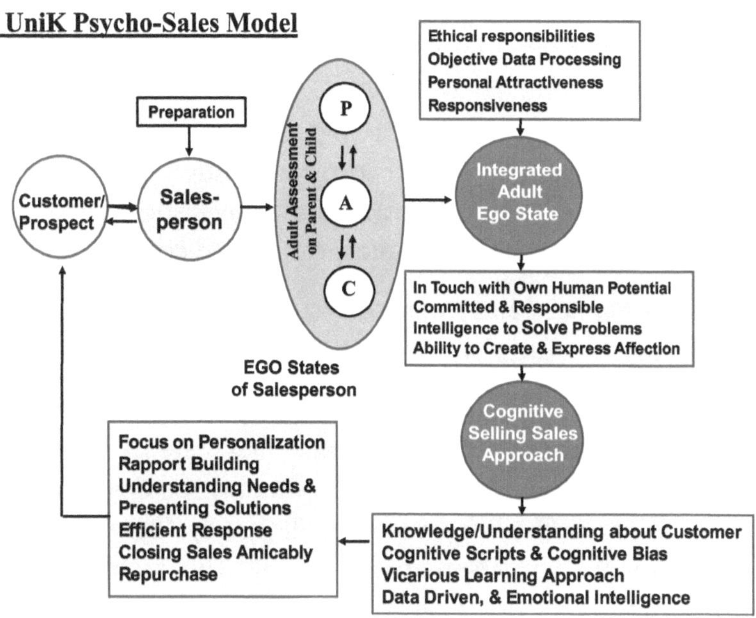

Figure 32: UniK Psycho-Sales Model

Welcome to the UniK Psycho-Sales Model!

"UniK" is a thoughtful abbreviation of my name, Unnikrishnan. This model is close to my heart, having evolved from over three decades of experience selling office furniture in Bahrain. My exposure to Counselling and Transactional Analysis was instrumental in integrating psychological insights with Cognitive selling.

I have diagrammatically presented the different stages of the UniK Psycho-Sales Model to help readers visualise and better understand it.

This sales model was designed to sell office furniture. However, it can be applied to products that benefit from cognitive selling techniques and personalised interactions. Office furniture is a complex product. Its specifications and detailing make it a diverse product. These are considered fixed assets, and organisations spend time and energy making purchase decisions. A competent salesperson bridges the connection between the customer and the company, influencing purchasing decisions. This model helps salespersons adopt an Integrated Adult ego state to make cognitive selling techniques effective and strengthen understanding between the salespersons and customers.

The UniK Psycho-Sales Model is a structured framework that utilises psychological principles to enhance sales effectiveness and efficiency. It consists of the following steps:

1. **Preparation**: This is the first step, requiring salespersons to prepare thoroughly before meeting a prospect. Benjamin Franklin said, "By failing to prepare, you are preparing to fail." This highlights the importance of preparation. Preparation is important:

   a. To qualify the prospect before the first meeting. Understand the prospects before we deal with them. This information can be collected from the company's website, social media, industry reports, initial phone calls, and other sources.

      We get inquiries from different prospects. Some may not be genuine; they want a quotation or proposal for comparison. It is better to avoid such customers diplomatically.

Customers may not have the financial capacity to afford our products or solutions, or our products may not be relevant to their needs.

Thus, qualifying the customer before the first meeting will help the salesperson avoid embarrassing situations and make the meeting productive and successful.

b. Manage Time. Time is precious in business. It helps to focus on the most promising prospects and spend time with them. Time should be used effectively in sales.

c. Know the right person. It is crucial to connect with the right person or decision-maker within an organisation. The salesperson should get this information before the first meeting. Knowing the background of the prospects will help develop rapport.

d. To help with the presentation. A well-prepared presentation exhibits professionalism and draws the attention of prospects. The ideas will be presented confidently using the proper presentation documents or catalogues, proving that you respect the prospect's time and are serious about their requirements.

I have observed prospects seeking meaningful exchanges of information that can economically address their problems when purchasing B2B products. In such cases, sales professionals should maintain intelligent conversations, which require thorough preparation and practice. Thus, through proper preparation, a salesperson can expect a fruitful first meeting, which in turn leads to effective interactions with prospects.

2. **Meetings:** The phrase "the first impression is the best impression" is a common proverb. However, I would like to add that the first impression should not only be the

best but also a lasting one. If a salesperson can achieve this, half the battle will be won, and the stage will be set for a strong relationship.

We examine the dynamics of human interaction through the Transactional Analysis psychological framework, making meetings more meaningful and successful.

When a salesperson interacts with a prospect or customer, six ego states may be in play: the salesperson's Parent, Adult, and Child, as well as the prospect's Parent, Adult, and Child. Each ego state has a distinct way of thinking, feeling, and behaving.

Below are examples of typical words, voice tones, behaviours, and attitudes expressed by the different ego states during communication (Berne, 2016). For better clarity on the ego states, I have considered the two divisions of the Parent ego state—Controlling Parent and Nurturing Parent—and the two divisions of the Child ego state—Adapted Child and Free Child.

Ego state	Typical words/ phrases	Typical voice tone	Typical behaviour	Typical attitudes
Controlling Parent (**CP**)	That is disgraceful. You Should. Because I said so. Don't you dare.	Angry. Sharp. Commanding. Critical. Judging. Impatient.	Furrowed brow. Point Finger. Giving orders. Criticising. Lecturing.	Judgemental. Authoritarian. Criticising. Punishing. Inflexible.
Nurturing Parent (**NP**)	I will take care of it for you. I am here for you. I believe in you.	Sympathetic. Encouraging. Empathetic. Kind.	Consoling touch. Being patient. Providing comfort.	Caring. Loving. Understanding. Helping. Protective. Encouraging.

Ego state	Typical words/ phrases	Typical voice tone	Typical behaviour	Typical attitudes
Adult (**A**)	When? What? Why? How? I understand. Let us analyse the facts.	Calm. Enquiring. Steady. Neutral. Clear. Precise. Analytical.	Relaxed. Attentive. Aware. Eye Contact. Open-minded. Problem-solving.	Non-judgemental. Fair & Balanced. Analytical. Pragmatic. Objective. Logical.
Adapted Child (**AC**)	I will try hard. Thank you. Please. Is this OK? I am sorry.	Submissive. Obedient. Apologetic.	Downcast eyes. Obeying orders. Avoiding conflict. Seeking approval.	Passive. Afraid. Guilty. Eager to please everyone.
Free Child (**FC**)	That is great. Let us have some fun. I feel so happy. So exciting.	Expressive. Excited. Joyful. Innocent. Curious.	Clear demonstration of feelings. Curiosity. Creativity. Being Authentic.	Spontaneous. Curious. Loving. Creative. Open. Playful. Enjoying freedom.

Table 9: Ego States and Modes of Communication

It is evident from the above chart that a salesperson should be able to operate from different ego states depending on the situation. To enhance a purposeful sales interaction, the ego states can be used as detailed below:

Adult Ego state: During the meeting, the salesperson operates from an Adult ego state under the following situations:

a. Gathering Information: To learn more details about the company, the decision-makers, the type of products they are looking for, the budget allocation for the product, and product specifications, such as the colour of the chair, the type of upholstery, or the arms or base.

b. Presenting the product or solution: Explain how a particular product (Chair) will be suitable for the prospect, present the facts and figures about the chair, and logically justify the quality of the chair through Test Certificates, warranty, and testimonials from the existing users of the chair.

c. Responding to objections: No salesperson will claim they never faced objections during a sale. They are common and must be handled prudently with logic and evidence. For example, customers may object to the product's performance. This objection can be addressed by offering an extended warranty to ensure long-term reliability and provide for after-sales service.

d. Commercial Terms: This is important in sales. Pricing, terms, and conditions should be meticulously calculated to avoid losses. The focus should be on information, not assumptions.

e. Closing the sale: A sale can be finalised only when the salesperson and the customer agree. This requires transparent, rational, and genuine communication from the Adult ego state.

Adult ego states can manage, coordinate and balance the Parent and Child ego states, ensuring professional interaction.

Parent Ego State: The Parent ego state has two divisions: Nurturing and Controlling. The salesperson wisely adopts these subdivisions in a meeting to establish authority and provide help, care, and guidance.

Nurturing Parent Ego State: A salesperson behaves from this ego state when creating a helpful and supportive atmosphere is desired. This ego state gets activated under the following circumstances.

a. Rapport Building: This is crucial in sales, as it makes prospects feel comfortable and respected. When a customer complains about the discomfort they experience in their current chair, the salesperson shows empathy by saying, "I can understand your discomfort with your current chair." Back pain makes our lives difficult. We offer a range of ergonomic chairs specifically designed to alleviate back and neck pain, featuring specially designed lumbar and neck support.

b. Providing guidance: Salespersons should help customers make informed decisions, enabling them to solve their problems using the products effectively. This is possible when salespersons show concern for customers' needs.

c. Positive Experience: Empathy, desire to help, and trust create a positive and memorable experience for customers. Purchasing with zero risk and assurance from the salesperson can build long-term customer connections.

Controlling Parent Ego State: This ego state should be used with caution. This approach has some benefits in sales and can be suitable; for example, if a customer is confused about choosing the right chair from the range of chairs, a Controlling Parent ego state salesperson can authoritatively say, 'This is the best ergonomic chair suitable for you. The features of this chair exactly solve your problems.' This strong advice may prompt the customer to purchase. This ego state is characterised by being authoritative and, therefore, can be used to communicate rules and regulations, as well as provide expert advice and assurance.

The Nurturing and Controlling Parent ego states should be balanced to make sales effective.

Child Ego State: The Child ego state is our 'felt' concept of life. A salesperson adopts this ego state to behave emotionally and exhibit feelings such as happiness, excitement, fear, frustration, or anger. The Child ego state has two divisions: Natural Child and Adapted Child.

Natural Child Ego State: A salesperson adopting this ego state exhibits spontaneous, emotional, and creative behaviours. When it comes to selling, the Natural Child ego state helps in the following way:

a. Approach customers in a friendly manner, creating a welcoming environment that makes them feel comfortable and encourages them to engage more effectively.

b. In this ego state, a salesperson will be flexible and spontaneous, able to adapt to different situations, making the sales process more entertaining and memorable.

c. To transfer the enthusiasm and excitement about a product to customers, creating a favourable purchasing situation.

d. Creatively overcome customers' objections. Finding creative solutions may tilt the balance in the salesperson's favour and aid in the purchasing process.

e. To make the product features and benefits colourful and easily understandable through their lively presentations.

When selling a chair, if the customer asks about its durability, I sometimes adopt the Child ego state and answer metaphorically to convey its durability. I say, "You may retire from the company, but not this chair." This convinces the customer that the chair is built to last.

Adapted Child Ego State: When a salesperson adopts an Adapted Child ego state in their sales approach, they behave according to the internalised societal norms and expectations. The Adapted Child ego state helps in the following way:

a. They strictly adhere to the company's rules and regulations and are willing to collaborate to find solutions.

b. They are respectful, polite, and courteous towards customers. This helps build rapport, as the customer feels valued, knowing that their opinions and preferences are respected.

c. They avoid challenging or conflicting situations.

However, one should be careful about the negative aspects of the Adapted ego state. They might exhibit a lack of assertiveness, fear of rejection, passive behaviour, overly compliance with the customer's requests, and lack of assertiveness. In summary, the Child ego state can be a valuable tool for selling. Balancing the Free and Adapted Child ego states and combining them with assertiveness and empathy can lead to a more well-rounded and practical approach to sales.

Balancing Ego States: During a sales interaction, the salesperson should be able to recognise and transition between Parent, Adult, and Child ego states as needed, depending on the situation. Each ego state has its unique strengths, leading to a more effective sales experience when utilised appropriately. The focus should be on operating from the Adult ego state, while also incorporating elements from the Nurturing Parent and Free Child ego states to foster rapport and enthusiasm. Thus, understanding and balancing the ego states helps salespersons and prospects communicate purposefully and successfully in sales interactions.

Types of Transactions: Understanding the various types of transactions enables the salesperson to comprehend the communication dynamics.

1. **Complementary Transactions**:

   In complementary transactions, the communication exchange is smooth, and the response is as expected. This is the ideal type of communication in sales as it results in:

   a. Effective communication as one receives the expected responses. The conversation becomes smooth and at the same wavelength as the stimulus and response are aligned.

   b. Continuous conversation: The conversation can continue without emotional outbursts, hurt feelings, or conversation stoppers. This means that salespersons can effectively explain themselves, make informed decisions, and create effective plans, among other benefits.

   c. Mutual understanding: The salesperson and prospects feel seen, respected, and understood. They are both in an OK position.

   d. Efficiency as the transactions lead to a productive exchange of information, resulting in the resolution of issues.

   For example:

   - Salesperson (Adult to Adult): "This chair features adjustable lumbar support, which helps support your back." Are you looking for this particular feature in the chair?

- Customer (Adult to Adult): "Yes, I was looking for this type of lumbar support in the chair. This is a perfect back support for me."

In complementary transactions, both parties reach a mutual agreement.

2. **Crossed Transactions**: This occurs when a salesperson receives an unexpected or different response that does not align with their initial expectation. Such interactions disrupt the communication flow, leading to:

a. Misunderstandings and disputes because the customer's concerns are inadequately handled.

b. Conflicts arise when the salesperson's tone or language does not align with customer expectations.

c. This is an obstacle to establishing trust and rapport, as the customer perceives the interaction as inauthentic and not genuine.

For example:

Customer (Adult ego state): "Can you give a warranty on the upholstery of this chair?"

Salesperson (Parent ego state): "Nobody gives a warranty on upholstery. You should focus on the seating comfort and not the upholstery."

In this case, the customer may feel frustrated because the query about the upholstery is not addressed.

Crossed transactions may lead to lost sales.

3. **Ulterior Transactions**: In such transactions, people often do not say what they mean. Two messages are communicated simultaneously: one on a social level (the spoken words) and another on a psychological level (the underlying meaning). In Ulterior transactions, the salesperson tries to manipulate customers by conveying hidden messages they would rather not disclose openly. It is essential to understand how the other person perceives the message. If these messages are not well received, it may harm the relationship.

   Example.

   Customer (Adult ego state): What is the cost of this chair?

   Salesperson (Adult ego state): Sir, this is an expensive brand chair.

   Ulterior Transaction (Parent to Child): You cannot afford the price.

If the customer receives the above message from the Child ego state, they attempt to challenge the statement: "I am not so poor; I can afford this chair" and tend to purchase the chair. If the Adult ego state receives the message, the customer thinks logically and concludes that the chair is expensive and beyond their budget.

Ulterior transactions should be used ethically and strategically. Salespersons should maintain transparency and genuineness in their sales transactions to foster long-term relationships.

Transactional Dynamics in Sales:

In Transactional Analysis theory, a sales meeting is an interaction between the ego states of the salesperson and the prospect. The question is, from which ego state should the salesperson start the meeting? Our research showed that "Salesperson's Ability to Identify the Customer's Requirements" ranked first. This comes from the Adult ego state. This ego state helps the salesperson gather information about the prospects objectively, ask fact-based questions about their requirements, and understand their needs precisely.

This approach may lead to an Adult-to-Adult transaction if the prospect also responds from an Adult ego state. This can facilitate complementary transactions, and the conversations can continue to yield the desired results. However, there may be situations where prospects do not respond from the same ego state. They may respond from the Critical Parent or Adapted Child ego state. This becomes a challenge for the salesperson.

Situation 1 - Salesperson in Adult and Prospect in Critical Parent:

In the Adult ego state, the salesperson takes a rational and logical position. However, the prospect in the Critical Parent ego state may negatively approach the product or salesperson, emphasising the product's shortcomings and dismissing the information provided. In such a situation, the salesperson should adopt the Adult ego state, remain calm, and refrain from reacting emotionally. Listen to the prospect patiently, acknowledge his concern, and explore the reasons behind his feelings. Focus on facts and figures to address his concerns, clarify his doubts, and lead the prospects to a solution-focused approach.

The salesperson can ask the questions listed below to solve the situation.

- I understand that you are concerned about our high price. Could you please let me know your target price so I can suggest products that align with your budget?

- I can see you are looking for products with higher specifications. Our product range encompasses a variety of models, so let us explore how we can tailor our offerings to meet your specific needs.

- Please let me know how we can best meet your requirements.

The primary objective is to help the prospect adopt an Adult ego state, enabling the transaction to become Adult-to-Adult and productive.

Situation 2 - Salesperson in Adult and Prospect in Adapted Child:

As mentioned earlier, in the Adult ego state, the salesperson will approach the situation rationally, non-judgementally, and logically. However, the prospect in the Adapted Child ego state may behave differently depending on the Adapted Child +ve or –ve. In the Adapted Child +ve, they may be obedient and seek approval or validation from the salesperson. In the –ve mode, they become rebellious or defiant. Here also, the salesperson should behave from the Adult ego, remain calm, ask questions to understand the prospect's needs, address the concerns or worries, provide information, and offer solutions as given below:

- I understand you find it difficult to decide without your management's approval. How can I assist you in obtaining the approval?

- What additional information do you require to make you more confident in decision-making?

- I can understand your frustration. I appreciate your patience. I am here to support you. Why not let us address your concerns?

The above process helps the salesperson in the Adult ego state take control of the situation and move the discussion forward.

Ego State Shifts

The survey shows that successful salespersons have all ego states active. In sales transactions, although Adult and Nurturing Parent ego states are powerful, elements of the Free Child ego state also play a role. The ability to shift the ego state to cater to the requirements of the situation is important, as detailed below:

- The Adult ego state plays an important role during negotiations, logical discussions, and providing information and details.

- Nurturing the Parent ego state helps build relationships and demonstrate understanding and concern for prospects. These are essential for building trust and long-term relationships.

- The Free Child ego state helps inject energy, enthusiasm, passion, and creativity, making discussions enjoyable and memorable.

Thus, effective communication requires shifting between ego states as needed by the demands of the interaction. The Adult ego state balances the Child and Parent ego states to ensure decisions are made comprehensively.

The development of the Adult ego is significant for a salesperson. Once this ego state is developed, the person can make decisions rationally, logically, and objectively. The adult ego state can be further developed into the Integrated Adult ego state, where the logical and rational aspects are combined with the nurturing and authoritative aspects of the parent, as well as the energy and creative aspects of the child.

From this ego state, decisions are more holistic, emotionally intelligent, and balanced.

Some experienced salespersons learn to balance their logical abilities, emotional factors, and creativity by handling diverse situations. Such individuals quickly develop an Integrated Adult ego state. Others can develop it through conscious effort, practice, professional training, mindfulness, and meditation.

In this sales model, the following factors are considered for developing the Integrated Adult ego state:

1. **Ethical Responsibilities**: Moral qualities and ethical responsibilities often originate from parents, including the rules and norms of society, as well as the concepts of what is right and wrong, mannerisms, and value systems that we learn from our parents and parental figures.

   Ethical responsibilities to guide our behaviour and decision-making can be developed in the following ways:

   A. Respect the privacy of others. Take proper consent or approval from others before disclosing confidential information.

   B. Present information honestly, accurately, and comprehensively.

   C. Treat people equally without bias and favouritism.

   D. People have value and dignity. Deal with them with respect and courtesy.

   E. Ensure that our behaviour aligns consistently with our moral principles and ethical standards.

F. Be accountable and responsible for our actions and decisions.

G. Ensure that our actions do not cause physical, emotional, or financial harm to others.

H. Ensure that individuals are fully aware of the results or risks associated with their decision before they express their consent.

I. Address those situations where personal interests conflict with professional duties.

J. Consider the long-term effect of our actions on the environment and future generations.

These ethical considerations help individuals and organisations make decisions that are not only legally compliant but also morally sound and socially responsible (MacKinnon, 2010).

2. **Objective Data Processing**: This contributes to developing the Integrated Adult ego state, as objective data processing enables us to respond effectively to present reality. The Adult collects information from outside sources and checks the relevance of the Child's reaction and the Parent's ideas to the present situation. The purpose is to obtain Adult integration to promote autonomy.

The objective data processing ability can be developed in the following ways:

a. Understand the characteristics, roles, and functions of Parent, Adult, and Child ego states. Focus on how the Adult takes charge of decision-making.

b. Make decisions logically and rationally, avoiding emotions or past conditioning. This is possible by processing data from the Adult ego state. Emotional decisions can lead to regrets and guilt.

c. Since decisions are made based on information or data, the reliability of data or information is important. The reliability of the data source or information should be established before incorporating it into the decision-making process, ensuring that the decisions are informed and reliable.

d. Cognitive biases will hurt rational decision-making. Identify such biases and overcome them. Challenge irrational beliefs. Verify whether our rational beliefs are indeed rational.

e. Practice techniques such as mindful breathing, mindful walking, mindful listening, and mindful meditation to enhance our focus on the present moment.

f. Evaluations are beneficial for improvements and are conducted by experienced and knowledgeable individuals. We should seek help from trusted experts to improve our decision-making process.

g. Continuous learning is an asset for our development. Update and upgrade our knowledge through continuous learning.

Practising the above steps enhances our ability to handle data without bias and make more informed choices.

3. **Personal Attractiveness**: These qualities are associated with the (Free) Child ego state. The qualities of the Free Child ego state, such as openness, playfulness, joyfulness, sense of humour, and spontaneity, make them accessible and attractive. Salespersons with personal attractiveness create a positive image and make social interactions attractive.

Salespersons can increase their attractiveness in the following ways:

a. By demonstrating assertiveness. An appealing salesperson who wins customers' attention is someone with a pleasant smile who meets potential clients eye-to-eye, speaks clearly while explaining the product, and offers viable solutions to anticipated challenges.

b. By demonstrating an understanding of customers' needs, a prudent salesperson thoroughly understands the customers' needs to provide them with a suitable solution through the products offered. This approach enhances the bond with the customer. Empathy is the bridge between the sales interaction and the customer relationship.

c. By taking care of health. A healthy lifestyle leads to a healthy appearance, increased energy level, better physical and mental health, and inspires others. All these increase the personal attractiveness of a salesperson.

d. Focus on self-improvement. Self-improvement is important for a salesperson to remain competitive in the field. It demands learning new skills, understanding objectives, personal development, and cultivating a growth mindset.

Thus, personal attractiveness helps salespersons to create a positive impression on customers, leading to rational decision-making.

4. **Responsiveness**: Responsiveness, in simple terms, refers to a person's ability to respond quickly and positively to a stimulus. When a person responds logically, rationally, and objectively from the Adult ego state, combining

the nurturing and supporting characteristics of the Parent ego state with the spontaneity and emotional expression of the Child ego state, they are likely to exhibit characteristics of the Integrated Adult.

To develop responsiveness, a salesperson can adopt the following steps:

a. Listen actively and uninterrupted to understand the customer's problems and requirements. Respond to show your involvement in the discussion.

b. Acknowledge the customer's concerns and respond empathetically.

c. Communicate using simple language so that customers understand quickly.

d. Time is an important factor. Respond quickly to show your interest and seriousness.

e. Make responsiveness an integral part of sales. Promptly respond to emails, messages, and missed calls to show respect to the sender.

f. Respond from the appropriate ego state to make the transactions complementary.

A salesperson can win customers by including the above steps in the sales process.

An example of a salesperson responding from the Integrated Adult ego state is explained below:

A customer plans to purchase a high-end chair for his staff but is unsure whether it will address their needs and meet his budget.

1. The salesperson responds from the Adult ego state by being logical, rational, and objective.

The salesperson listens carefully to the customer's pain points, requirements, and budget constraints.

The salesperson understands the customer's requirements and provides detailed and accurate information about the chair's specifications, features, and benefits. The salesperson also justifies the chair's quality with test certificates and provides a warranty.

Shows chairs of other models with the exact specifications that might suit the customer's needs.

2. The salesperson responds from the Parent ego state by nurturing and supporting behaviour.

The customer is unconvinced about his staff accepting the same chair and is concerned that it may exceed the budget. The salesperson understands the customer's hesitation about accepting the chair and their budget concerns.

The salesperson empathises with and understands the customer's concerns, offering reassurance. They offer supportive suggestions and guidance to help customers make informed decisions.

Salesperson: It is important to select the right chair, or it may lead to health problems for staff. Compromising on the quality is not the right decision. Here is a product that lasts long, and the price is lower when spread over the years. Go for quality and be confident in your purchase. We are here to support your decision. We can arrange a trial period to allow all your staff to experience the comfort of sitting in the chair. Once they are satisfied, you can place the order.

Price is related to the value you get. However, we can offer flexible payment options for orders with a minimum quantity to reduce the financial burden. Remember, this chair is an investment in the comfort and well-being of your staff, which in turn increases their productivity.

3. The salesperson responds from the Child ego state (Spontaneity and Emotional Expression):

Here, the salesperson responds with excitement and emotion. They make the interaction more engaging to create an emotional connection with the chair.

Salesperson: Wow! This chair's durability is such that even if you retire, it will not. It will continue to perform. I have personal experience with this chair, and I am using the same model. It has made a world of difference for me. You deserve this comfortable chair. This is a great choice. Make your life comfortable!

Combining ethical responsibilities (Ethos), objective data processing (Logos), personal attractiveness, and responsiveness (Pathos) can indeed contribute to the development of an Integrated Adult ego state in a salesperson. Thus, salespersons evaluate information objectively during their interactions with prospects or customers and behave with respect and integrity. This makes interactions more attractive by creating a positive image that strengthens personal bonds.

Once a salesperson operates from an Integrated Adult ego state, they exhibit the following qualities that enhance their professional and personal effectiveness.

a. In touch with the salesperson's potential. Salespersons understand their skills, balance their ego states, and specifically select the ego state that is most appropriate for engagement in an interaction. This is particularly relevant in sales because it enables effective communication and the building and maintenance of strong relationships.

b. Committed and Responsible: This occurs when salespersons assume the Adult ego state, becoming sensible, rational, and practical in their approach. This brings a sense of commitment and responsibility. They become committed to awareness and personal growth. At the professional level, they do not give up. They remain committed to meeting sales targets and improving customer satisfaction. They become interested in the products sold, inspire confidence in prospects, and support company goals.

Salespersons operating from the Adult ego state take responsibility, own their actions, and learn from their failures, rectifying them as needed. They become reliable, meet their commitments, and contribute to organisational success.

c. Intelligence to solve problems: The Adult ego state prepares the salesperson to analyse data and situations logically and objectively. This will help them to find the root cause of the problems. They evaluate various options and make informed decisions. Thus, the Integrated Adult ego state combines rational analysis, creative thinking, ethical behaviour, and enthusiasm to solve problems and achieve successful sales outcomes.

d. Ability to create and express affection: Salespersons, in their Integrated Adult ego, understand and empathise with their customers' needs and feelings. This helps them develop rapport and connect with customers. The characteristics of an Integrated Adult ego state, such as active listening, positive and encouraging words, customised solutions, honesty, and transparency, win customers' hearts.

Thus, salespersons operating from the Integrated Adult ego state function by integrating valuable information from the Parent and Child ego states. They interact with customers in a logical, objective, and mature manner. Results: communication becomes effective, listening becomes active, and problem-solving becomes logical. Combining this with the above qualities – A salesperson's potential, commitments, and responsibilities, intelligence to solve problems, and ability to create and express affection creates a strong framework for Cognitive Selling. Hence, a salesperson is equipped to switch to a Cognitive selling sales approach effortlessly in the following way:

a. By gaining knowledge and understanding of customers: The study showed that "listening to customers' concerns" (Rank 1) and "Gathering information about customers' needs and preferences" (Rank 2) are important components of Cognitive selling. These two factors are crucial for customising solutions or recommending suitable products to customers. The mature interaction from the Adult ego state enables the salesperson to identify and understand the customer's pain points, address their specific needs, provide tailor-made solutions, and build long-lasting relationships.

b. Cognitive Scripts & Cognitive Bias:

Cognitive selling scripts outline the step-by-step procedures to follow during sales interactions, guiding salespersons to navigate various sales situations and achieve success effectively. Since Integrated Adult can integrate various aspects of personality, they will be able to design a sales script that adapts to customers' needs and provides a positive sales experience. The Cognitive sales scripts from an Integrated Adult ego state have the following features:

a. A balanced assessment of information leads to a rational and practical sales script.

b. The scripts focus on the present moment, free from past biases and future anxieties.

c. The problem-solving ability of the Integrated Adult ego state develops a script to offer solutions to difficult sales situations.

d. By balancing the ego states, the script reduces stress in high-pressure sales situations.

Thus, the Integrated Adult ego state in Cognitive selling scripts leads to improved sales results.

Cognitive biases are systematic and predictable judgement errors we make (Tsipursky, 2020). They are mental shortcuts that lead to wrong decisions. The Integrated Adult ego state can help overcome these biases in the following ways:

1. By encouraging the salespeople to analyse the situation logically without the interference of emotions and preconceived notions.

2. By focusing on the present, decisions can be made based on current information.

3. By questioning the assumptions and looking for alternative solutions.

4. By managing their emotions, salespeople can remain calm and rational even in difficult situations.

5. By thinking outside the box and remaining open-minded, a salesperson considers new options and ideas to suit the present situation.

The Integrated Adult ego state plays a significant role in forming Cognitive scripts and overcoming Cognitive biases, helping to improve sales.

Vicarious Learning Approach: Vicarious learning is a form of observational learning. This is an efficient way to learn, as beginners gain practical exposure to selling from experienced and successful salespeople. They can avoid the mistakes committed by experienced or successful salespersons.

When a salesperson is in the Integrated Adult ego state, their thought process is present-focused, analytical, and rational. This helps them to remain focused, objective, and logical while learning. They can make thoughtful decisions and conclusions based on observations. They avoid repeating their own mistakes and those of others. Vicarious learning becomes more effective due to a deeper understanding of practical strategies and sales methods.

The knowledge gained from vicarious training can refine cognitive skills. Cognitive scripts can include the proven techniques practised by successful salespersons to handle objections, build rapport, and close deals. All these help evolve and refine cognitive scripts to be up to date.

Vicarious learning is a common practice in many organisations. Mr. Sunil joined ABC Office Furniture Company as a Sales Trainee. Initial training focuses on imparting knowledge of the company's products, including their features, benefits, value proposition, competitive advantage, and the services provided to various market segments. Product knowledge makes a salesperson confident.

Next, Mr. Sunil is allowed to use the product to get hands-on experience. He sits in different chairs to experience the comfort of sitting and checks the details of the desks. This experience is crucial for understanding the product from the customer's perspective and clarifying their doubts.

Mr. Sunil has good product knowledge and is fit to meet customers' needs. Instead of sending him alone to the market, he accompanies his manager to sales meetings. This is to observe the tips and tricks of sales, presentation methods, customer interaction, objection handling, and closing techniques. This vicarious learning will enable Mr. Sunil to become a competent salesperson.

In addition, Mr. Sunil will be given role-playing exercises to practice selling, handling objections, and improving communication skills. He will also receive ongoing training sessions to further his selling acumen, where product developments, industry trends, and best practices will be updated.

Incorporating vicarious learning leads to continuous improvements in cognitive selling, resulting in successful sales outcomes.

Data-driven: This means that the decision-making process is guided by information, rather than assumptions. This originates from the Adult ego state, where decisions and actions are based on the analysis and interpretation of data, ensuring the outcome remains unbiased, quantifiable, and realistic. This will help salespersons to make informed decisions, identify prospects, tailor their selling strategies, and overcome cognitive biases. For example, some purchasers prefer detailed information on products. In such cases, the salesperson should be equipped with in-depth product details and a clear understanding of the competitive advantages of the products under consideration. Test certificates of products provide proof of product quality. They can be used to counteract biases such as confirmation bias (confirming pre-existing beliefs) and anchoring bias (relying too heavily on the first piece of information received).

Emotional Intelligence: For salespersons, Emotional Intelligence enables them to recognise, understand, manage, and effectively utilise emotions in themselves and their customers (NeuroLaunch.com, 2024). This enables salespersons to connect with customers on a profound level. A salesperson who has high Emotional Intelligence can:

a. Understand customers' emotions and build connections, as customers desire salespersons who acknowledge their expectations.

b. Control their emotions during critical situations and maintain productive and positive communication.

c. Handle objections and conflicts because they understand the emotions behind them and can convert those setbacks into opportunities.

d. Foster long-term relationships with customers by crafting emotionally resonant messages that resonate with their values.

e. Stay motivated and resilient by maintaining a consistently positive outlook.

A salesperson can manage emotions and resolve conflicts to make an approach more personalised, thereby building trust in them.

The responses of a salesperson with emotional intelligence under different situations are illustrated below:

Salesperson (Empathetic Response): "I am sorry to find that you are suffering from back pain due to the wrong sitting posture. I can see that you are upset, and I'm here to help resolve the issue as quickly as possible. Can you tell me more about the problem so we can find the best solution together?"

Salesperson (Personal Connection and Encouragement): "I agree that choosing the right product can be overwhelming. Let us take our time to find something that fits your needs perfectly. I recommend this ergonomic chair with a three-lever mechanism to adjust the angle between the seat and back, adjustable lumbar support, seat depth adjustment, adjustable arms and neck support, and a mesh back. Moreover, this is warranted for a period of ten years. Many could overcome their back pain with this chair. This chair will be beneficial to you."

Salesperson (Understanding and Offering Solutions): "I understand that pricing is an obstacle in purchasing this chair. I know you will appreciate that the price is always related to the value you get. This chair is warranted for ten years and is expected to perform beyond this period. We do offer financing schemes to make this purchase more comfortable. Additionally, we have a festival offer next week, and you can benefit from it."

Salesperson (Confidence and Reassurance): "I appreciate your decision to purchase the chair. If you are not satisfied with this chair, you can return it within five days and receive a full refund. For any clarifications, please do not hesitate to contact me. Enjoy sitting and working."

Thus, a salesperson with emotional intelligence takes the customer into confidence empathetically and builds trust and long-lasting relationships.

The Integrated Adult Ego is a rainbow of all ego states wherein the Adult aspect plays the colouring role. In this ego state, a salesperson becomes more logical and rational, providing solutions to problems while setting aside emotional factors. The characteristics of the Integrated Adult ego state align with the principles of Cognitive Selling, including understanding the customer, personalisation, rapport building, and providing ethical solutions rather than selling. This helps achieve sales success.

Personalisation: Customers like personalisation, which has become a hallmark of selling. It demonstrates that the salesperson takes a personal interest in resolving the customer's problems effectively, which increases the likelihood of purchasing and retaining customers.

Rapport Building: This is a crucial element in selling. It is a general observation that customers buy from someone they trust and like. This can lead to productive interactions, as the customers can open up to salespersons they feel comfortable with. They discuss without any barriers and arrive at quick and congenial decisions. A satisfied customer is an asset to a business, as they make repeat purchases and become valuable referrals.

Understanding Needs and Presenting Solutions: This is crucial for effective selling. Customers tend to reciprocate to salespersons who take a personal interest, spend time and effort understanding their needs, and offer the appropriate solution. This helps them appreciate the value of the product they have purchased, thereby enhancing their satisfaction and relationships.

Efficient Response: A salesperson who acts promptly without wasting time gains the customer's attention. Customers receive accurate information at the right time, enabling them to make informed decisions. Furthermore, salespeople can manage a greater number of clients in less time, thereby increasing their productivity.

Closing Sales Amicably: This is a crucial stage in the sales process. All salespersons look forward to this stage in their sales process. Closing sales amicably brings satisfaction to the customers and salespersons. Once the customer is aware of the pros and cons of the product they have purchased, there is no room for after-sales disputes. This is crucial in establishing long-term relationships. Satisfied customers support salespersons in promoting products in their social circle.

Repurchase: In sales, people focus on converting products into cash. However, it is better to take this step forward to inspire customers to come to us and make repeat purchases. Repurchasing helps steady cash flow at low marketing expenses, which is important for a company's success.

To conclude, when the Integrated Adult ego state integrates with the Cognitive selling principles, the sales process becomes harmonised, client-centred, and structured, leading to more successful and harmonious outcomes.

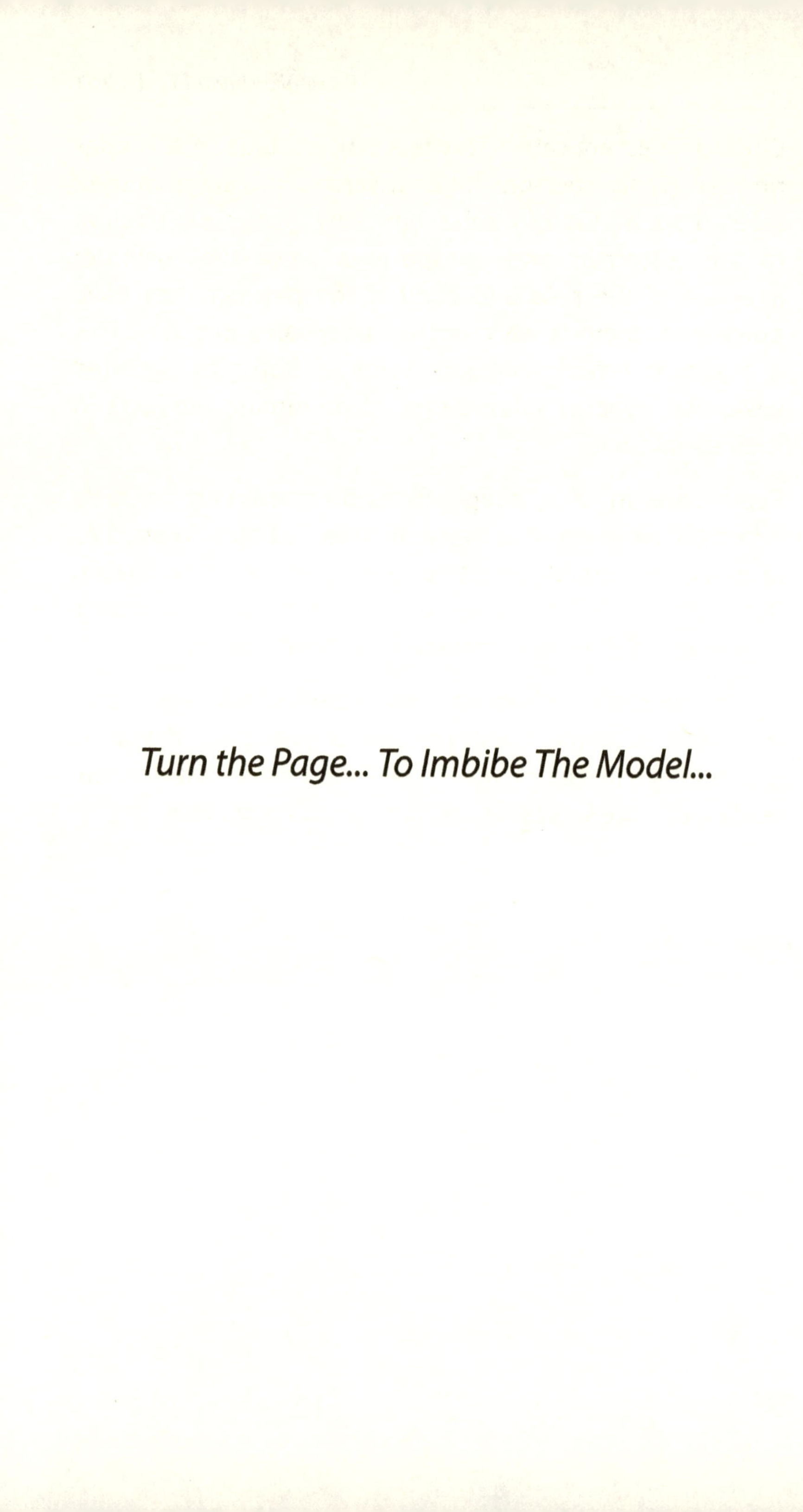
Turn the Page... To Imbibe The Model...

Chapter 11

Putting Principles into Practice

"It's not what we profess but what we practice that gives us integrity."

– Francis Chan

DEF is a multinational company with more than 1,000 employees. They regularly purchase Height-Adjustable Desks (HAD). Surprisingly, they have been buying only from ABC Furniture. This company has maintained the sole supplier position for HADs in DEF. The demand for this product is growing. A thought came to mind: why not sell our HAD to DEF? I was confident that a competent salesperson becomes the link between the company and the customer, influencing purchasing decisions. I worked on these lines.

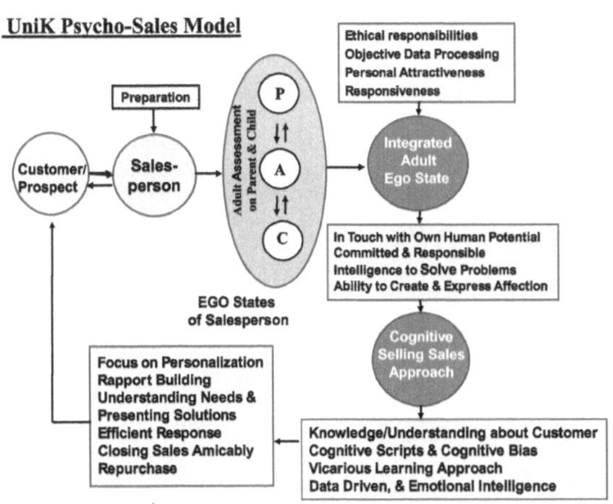

Figure 32: UniK Psycho-Sales Model

The subsequent sections illustrate a series of face-to-face conversations in which I used the principles of Transactional Analysis (TA) and Cognitive Selling (CS). TA was used to understand the underlying psychological dynamics in sales conversations, and CS was used to understand the client's thought processes and decision-making patterns. By putting the principles into practice, I could break the competitor's monopoly and gain entry into DEF.

The first step in the UniK Psycho-Sales Model is preparation (Adult ego state). From reliable sources, I gathered the following information. DEF was a multinational company. It had safety rules and took care of the welfare of its employees. The company had been in the country for three decades and wanted to expand its operations in this region. Typically, when a company undertakes expansion projects, it redesigns its existing office spaces to enhance efficiency and optimise space utilisation. It recruited new employees and required additional office space. This necessitated additional office furniture. Furniture suppliers could expect large orders or long-term contracts for office furniture. I realised that if we could close a deal with this company, they might opt for the same furniture for future expansions, allowing them to maintain the aesthetics and uniformity. In short, it was an opportunity I could not afford to miss, and it required building lasting relationships with DEF.

The question I faced was how to get in touch with this organisation (Adult ego state). In organised companies, the procurement department or purchasing department is responsible for purchasing office furniture. I visited their website and took the purchaser's contact details. I fixed an appointment with the Purchaser.

The snippets of our telephone conversations are given below:

Salesperson (Unni): Good morning, Mr. Anil. My name is Unni, and I am from MKT Office Furniture Company. How are you doing today? (Adult ego state).

Customer (Anil): I am fine. (Adult ego state).

Salesperson (Unni): Good to know that. I want to inform you that MKT specialises in ergonomic office furniture. Given a chance, we can bring a positive change to your office setting (Adult ego state).

Customer (Anil): It is good to hear that (Adult ego state).

Salesperson (Unni): Great. I recently learned that your company has expansion programmes (Adult ego state).

Customer (Anil): You are right. We intend to expand our operations within the country (Adult ego state).

Salesperson (Unni): I am happy to hear that. We can offer our services to make your office more comfortable, productive, and aesthetic (Adult ego state).

Customer (Anil): That is interesting (Adult ego state).

Salesperson (Unni): Thank you. However, I need to understand more about your requirements and the current setup under which employees work to provide you with an appropriate solution (Adult ego state).

Customer (Anil): Yes. It sounds logical (Adult ego state).

Salesperson (Unni): Is it possible to fix up a brief meeting to understand your specific needs? Could you give me an appointment at a convenient date and time? (Adult ego state).

Customer (Anil): Yes, it is possible. We can meet on Wednesday at 10 a.m. (Adult ego state).

Salesperson (Unni): Thank you. I look forward to meeting you. If the schedule changes, please inform me using my mobile number (Adult ego state).

In the introductory conversation, I operated from my Adult ego state as I was interested in gathering information from the customer. This ego state helped me focus on the information by remaining calm, rational, and objective in my approach, without becoming emotional or critical. I wanted to know whether the customer would be willing to discuss this with me initially. The customer also reciprocated from his Adult ego state, as he was interested in learning more about my company. We could maintain complementary transactions. The result was positive. Since I got an appointment for the first physical meeting with the customer, I prepared thoroughly, leaving no room for flaws. I prepared with the same seriousness as preparing for a job interview. I wanted to make the best use of this meeting. I aimed to impact the customer, fostering long-term relationships positively. This was possible only when my presentation was professional and flawless. I prepared catalogues featuring various models of height-adjustable desks, executive desks, and ergonomic chairs. I prepared the features and benefits of the products to explain why this furniture is the best for their employees. I prepared thoroughly to highlight the competitive advantages of my products, utilising test certificates and testimonials from satisfied customers. I knew even the best products at affordable prices would not sell unless the salesperson put an effort into selling. Now, the ball was in my court. It became my responsibility to effectively convey to customers the product's features, benefits, and competitive advantages, so that DEF would favour me with a contract. Yes, I was well prepared for the meeting and could visualise securing a contract from DEF.

Wednesday, the meeting day, dawned promising new opportunities. I was excited to meet Mr. Anil, the purchaser. My product knowledge and flawless preparation gave me the confidence and courage to impress Mr. Anil. I made it a point to be in the meeting room 10 minutes before 10 a.m. In the meeting, he was impressed by my product presentation. I emphasised the importance of ergonomic office furniture, highlighting how it promotes proper body posture, prevents back and neck pain, enhances collaboration, and fosters a pleasant work environment. He was satisfied with my products and their features and benefits.

The snippets of our conversations are given below:

Customer (Anil): Thank you for the information. Your products have good specifications and quality standards (Adult ego state).

Salesperson (Unni): Good to hear this! How can we proceed further? (Adult ego state).

Customer (Anil): Since this is a technical product, I cannot make the decisions alone. I screen the suppliers and forward the qualified ones to the Technical Manager for review and approval. He will evaluate the report and provide it to me; we will then decide whether to proceed with the purchase based on the findings. (Adult ego state).

Salesperson (Unni): Oh! If that is the procedure, please give the contact details of your Technical Manager. (Adult ego state).

Customer (Anil): I will inform the Technical Manager about our meeting. I have your contact details and the product catalogues. I will arrange a meeting with him next Tuesday at 10 a.m. (Adult ego state).

Salesperson (Unni): Thank you for your time. (Nurturing Parent ego state, as it shows politeness and appreciation.) It is lovely to talk to you (Nurturing Parent ego state). I look forward to a meeting with the Technical Manager (Adult ego state). Have a great day! (Nurturing Parent ego state - Courteous and positive closing).

After this meeting, I was very elated. I realised I was on the right track. My presentation was engaging, communication was clear and impressive, and my product knowledge proved my expertise, resulting in developing a good rapport with the customer. I learned a valuable lesson: Selling starts with the salesperson. The customer should accept the salesperson and then the product being sold.

As expected, my meeting with the Technical Manager was confirmed on Tuesday. I knew this meeting was very crucial for me. Typically, technical managers delve into the details of a product. I should be geared to answer all his questions about functionality, durability, and technical specifications. His decisions would carry more weight. This time, I started thinking from his perspective. Why should he buy from me? How could I justify this? Some of the areas I covered were as follows:

   a. Technical and Safety Factors of Height-Adjustable Desks.

   b. Test certificates and customer testimony.

   c. Datasheet of the product.

   d. Adaptability to their existing situations and aesthetics.

   e. Ergonomic benefits.

   f. Comparison with other products available in the market.

   g. After-sales service, warranty, and maintenance, etc.

I was well prepared for the meeting. As scheduled, I met with him on Tuesday at 10:00 a.m.

The snippets of my conversations with the Technical Manager are given below:

Salesperson (Unni): Good morning, Sir. My name is Unni, and I represent MKT. We specialise in ergonomic office furniture.

Technical Manager (Yogesh): Good morning. My name is Yogesh. I was expecting you.

Salesperson (Unni): That is nice to know. Last week, I met with your purchaser, Mr. Anil. He was pretty impressed with our products and suggested that I discuss them with you and obtain your approval.

Technical Manager (Yogesh): Mr. Anil informed me about you and your products. Frankly, we have been purchasing height-adjustable desks from ABC Furniture. We are pretty satisfied with this product. Why should I consider another model? (Cognitive bias is Status Quo bias).

Salesperson (Unni): I appreciate your perspective. I understand you are satisfied with your current desk and do not want to change it. This is quite common with people. Many of our customers also shared this sentiment before purchasing from us. May I take a look at your desk to evaluate it?

Technical Manager (Yogesh): Yes, sure. I do not mind.

The Technical Manager exhibited a "status quo bias," as he preferred to maintain the current state and was reluctant to change. He did not want to take any risk involved in a change. There was a possibility that he might have been influenced by the product pricing and features, which led to Anchoring bias.

I checked the existing desks. I wanted to compare them side by side to highlight how my desk would be ideal for the customer. I quickly jotted down some points that would appeal to his technical brain.

Salesperson (Unni): Thank you for the opportunity to evaluate your existing desk. I made a quick comparison between your current desk and ours. I can help you determine how our desks can offer more features and benefits. I would be delighted to demonstrate how our desks can provide even greater value for your team. Can I share a few unique benefits we offer?

Technical Manager (Yogesh): Yes. Let me hear.

Salesperson (Unni): Our height-adjustable desks are designed to promote better posture, reduce strain, and increase productivity. For example,

a. Our desks are available in various wood finishes and leg colours to complement your theme or decor.

b. It has four memory settings. This means one touch will adjust the height of the desks to four different heights, making them user-friendly.

c. Its maximum height is 125 cms. Even at its tallest height, it remains firmly in place.

d. It is warranted for 10 years, to ensure that issues are resolved and ensure smooth performance.

e. The legs have a classic square design. The beam that joins the two legs for additional support is placed away from the knee, providing more space for the leg to move.

f. The cables are concealed as it has a full-length integrated cable management tray and a built-in power supply.

g. I possess the technical data and test certificates that conform to quality standards.

Technical Manager (Yogesh): That is interesting. Do you make furniture layouts?

Salesperson (Unni): Yes. We have a design department where experts design layouts to match customers' requirements and ergonomic factors. Please let me know exactly what you require. I will give a solution (Adult ego state). I am here to help you (Nurturing Parent ego state).

Technical Manager (Yogesh): It is nice to know this. I have a room that I want to accommodate 20 height-adjustable desks, a conference room, a manager's cabin, and cabinets for storing 500 box files. I know this is a difficult job. The current supplier created a drawing that did not meet our satisfaction, as it had limitations. If you can do it, it will be great.

Salesperson (Unni): We can indeed accept this challenge. Please email the CAD drawing to me. I will submit it within two days.

Technical Manager (Yogesh): That is fine. I will wait for you.

This meeting was productive as I successfully changed the Technical Manager's perspective. Asking me to prepare a furniture layout indicated that I could sell myself, diluting his fear of making a change. I could overcome his Status Quo and Anchoring Bias with genuine information and logical reasoning. The customer appreciated my product knowledge and found value in my insights, which helped him shift his perspective. The product-to-product comparison revealed that the benefits of the new height-adjustable desk outweighed the comfort of sticking with the current desk.

As explained in the UniK Psycho-Sales Model, while selling, I ensured that I was ethically responsible, able to process data objectively, personally attractive, and responsive, as detailed below:

Ethically responsible:

- Provided accurate information, justified by a datasheet and quality standard certificates.

- Respected the customer and never spoke ill of the competitors' products.

- Maintained Transparency in dealings.

Objective Data Processing:

- Objectively evaluated the current height-adjustable desk.

- Made accurate and factual comparisons.

- Explained the benefits of the new desks logically.

Personal Attractiveness:

- Maintained punctuality.

- Dressed for the occasion and groomed well.

- Exhibited confidence in knowledge and used positive body language.

Responsiveness:

- Listened attentively to the customer and responded promptly.

- Willingness to serve the customer without loss of time.

- Being adaptable to customers' needs and requirements.

The above factors helped me operate from my Integrated Adult ego state. The Technical Manager set aside all cognitive biases once I presented my arguments logically, objectively, empathetically, nurturingly, and creatively. With this, his mindset changed in my favour. Since he expressed dissatisfaction with the layout prepared by the current supplier, it presented an opportunity for me to assist him and earn his approval and goodwill. I wanted my layout designed in a way that would serve his needs and foster a positive relationship.

When I adopted the Integrated Adult ego state, I could effectively balance my responses and develop the following qualities:

In Touch with My Own Human Potential: I could realise and utilise my strengths and abilities. I could understand the Technical Manager's satisfaction with the existing product and his initial decision not to purchase an alternative height-adjustable desk. I could enumerate my product's competitive advantage and tilt the balance in my favour.

Committed and Responsible: I was dedicated to my company and its customers. My commitment to my organisation was to drive sales growth and foster strong customer relationships. My commitment to the customer was to fulfil my promises and ensure their satisfaction through our products and services.

Intelligence to Solve Problems: I realised the importance of innate intelligence (intelligence inherent from birth), acquired intelligence (developed over time), technological intelligence (applying scientific principles to solve problems), and emotional intelligence (managing emotions effectively). This helped me to solve problems by thinking critically and suggesting the additional features available with the new height-adjustable desk.

Ability to Create and Express Affection: I could speak the Technical Manager's native language, creating a sense of familiarity and belongingness. This helped us open up and become closer. He could create meaningful connections when he felt I was genuine and worked in his favour.

Coming back, the Technical Manager's request for the furniture layout indicated his seriousness in considering a switch to buy from me. This was an opportunity that should not be missed. The relationship could be strengthened by designing a layout catering to all his requirements. My idea was to surpass his expectations. I adopted the Nurturing Parent ego state to extend support and care to the Technical Manager. A carefully designed layout considering all relevant parameters would showcase our expertise, dedication, and accountability to him. This would hook him onto my products and services.

I collaborated with the designer at my company to create a layout that met the requirements of the Technical Manager. The following were considered to create a flawless furniture layout.

a. The shape and dimensions of the rooms and the positions of doors, windows, columns, and beams were earmarked to determine the best furniture arrangements.

b. Avoided blocking windows, doors, and emergency exits.

c. Defined pathways to ensure free movement of employees in the room.

d. Placed the storage units against the wall wherever possible to conserve space, maintain stability, and ensure accessibility, taking into account that electrical switches, outlets, and other fixtures are not obstructed.

e. Ensured the power outlets were conveniently located and the cables were safely and neatly organised as the height-adjustable desks were electrically operated.

f. The conference room was adjacent to the manager's cabin for easy accessibility.

g. A clip-on partition or privacy screen was included for each desk for privacy. This was necessary as there were too many staff in the room.

By incorporating the above factors, we created a functional layout. We could accommodate 22 people in the room, exceeding his expectations and providing privacy to each employee.

This was a notable achievement, as we completed the layout within a day, not two days, as promised. I felt elated. I emailed the drawing to the Technical Manager. I gave him a day to review my drawing. The next day, I called him over the telephone. I was eager to get his feedback.

The snippets of my conversations over the telephone with the Technical Manager are given below:

Salesperson (Unni): Good morning, Sir. Yesterday, I emailed you the furniture layout we prepared. Considering the ergonomic factors, we could accommodate 22 desks in the room and include two more (Adult ego state).

Technical Manager (Yogesh): Good morning. I got your email. I noted that you managed to accommodate 22 desks. Your attention to detail is commendable. That is fantastic. This exceeds our requirements. (Adult ego state).

Salesperson (Unni): Thank you, Sir. We achieved this after careful planning and brainstorming. (Adult ego state).

Technical Manager (Yogesh): I could notice that. I appreciate your problem-solving skills. Incidentally, we have six divisions looking for height-adjustable desks. (Adult ego state).

Salesperson (Unni): Oh! That is excellent news. (Free Child ego state).

Technical Manager (Yogesh): Is it not wonderful? (Free Child ego state). To save time, I would like to arrange a meeting with you and the divisional heads soon. (Adult ego state).

Salesperson (Unni): Thank you. I appreciate your move. Please let me know the date and time of the meeting that is convenient for all. I look forward to meeting you all. (Adult ego state).

Of course, this was a positive development in my efforts to sell the height-adjustable desk. The requirements were multiplied, and I had a greater responsibility to sell to the divisional heads. My success in selling to the Technical Manager gave me the confidence to repeat the same process, which worked well. Then why not repeat it?

This time, to my surprise, I had to sell to a panel consisting of six divisional heads, a Technical Manager, and a Purchasing Manager. I was very much excited to face this challenge. My success with the Technical Manager, public speaking skills, and belief in the competitive advantage of our products gave me the confidence to face the panel. My preparation encompassed areas such as health benefits to the user, instructions for using the desk, durability, maintenance, safety standards, collaboration with existing furniture, and customer testimonials.

I was excited to face the audience and present my ideas in the meeting. It was a golden opportunity to sell to a group, and I believed it to be the most efficient way to make sales in a shorter amount of time. I was able to address all the queries from different members convincingly. Yes, I was successful. That was a moment to prove my expertise and take all of them to the next stage in selling.

The next stage was a live product demonstration. The idea was to help the customer see the height-adjustable desk in operation, experience its features and benefits, and provide hands-on experience to turn their interest into confidence to purchase the desk. Soon, a demo was arranged, and all divisional managers were allowed to interact with the desk. They operated the desk themselves to realise that adjusting the height from sitting to standing was smooth and effortless, and the desk remained stable at various heights. The memory settings further enhanced quick height adjustment.

One divisional manager wanted three monitors on the desk for all staff in his division. This required additional power sockets and cabling, which were quickly made possible due to our customisation options.

I explained the product well, and the customer had a live interaction with the desk. All doubts were clarified. The next step was to provide a formal proposal. An outline of the proposal is presented below (figures and details were deliberately not mentioned here):

Proposal for height-adjustable desks:

Product: Height-Adjustable Desk, Design of desk leg., Model number, Specification, Finish of desktop, colour of the adjustable leg, Number of sockets on desktop.

Drawing: A detailed drawing of the furniture layout for different divisions and a drawing of the height-adjustable desk detailing the measurements of various components.

Pricing: Unit price, Division-wise quantity of desks, Discount offered, Total Amount.

Terms and Conditions: Delivery Schedule, Warranty Statement, After-Sales Service.

Additional Services: Installation, Training, Ongoing Support.

The above proposal was submitted to Mr. Gopal, the Purchase Manager. I knew that a purchaser would decide only after a comparative study of similar proposals from the competitors. After two days of giving the purchaser time to review the proposal, I contacted him to check on the status and determine if he needed further clarification.

11.1 *"Negotiate to Get a Nod":*

In my research, 'Salesperson's ability to close the sale at mutually agreeable terms and conditions' ranked second. This is a crucial cognitive skill, as it involves various mental processes, including the analysis of constraints from both the customer and the seller, problem-solving ability, planning alternatives to arrive at a conclusion, decision-making, and emotional intelligence. A series of complementary communications occurs between the seller and the customer to reach a mutually beneficial agreement.

When I contacted the Purchase Manager, he said, "Your price was high." This statement is quite common in sales, as the purchaser seeks the maximum value for their money. According to the UniK Psycho-Sales Model, the Integrated Adult ego state and Cognitive Selling help salespersons sharpen their negotiation skills.

In the Integrated Adult ego state, salespersons remain objective, rational, logical, calm, and composed. They focus on information rather than assumptions, making their analysis more accurate. At the same time, they address the customer's requirements or queries in a timely and appropriate manner. They incorporate the positive elements of Parent and Child ego states.

Cognitive Selling focuses on understanding customers' thought processes, preferences, and decision-making patterns. Cognitive bias can be leveraged to a salesperson's advantage, helping them tailor their communication to resonate with customers' cognitive preferences.

Thus, combining the Integrated Adult ego state with the Cognitive Selling approach creates a powerful strategy for successful negotiation, which builds trust, solves problems, and achieves consensus.

The snippets of my conversations with the Purchase Manager are given below:

Salesperson (Unni): Good morning, I hope you are doing well. I submitted my proposal for the height-adjustable desk for all divisions. Were you able to go through it?

Purchase Manager (Gopal): Yes, I went through it. However, your price is significantly higher than that of other proposals. It has gone beyond our budget.

Salesperson (Unni): I understand that our pricing is above your budget, which concerns your company. However, budget constraints are quite a common challenge when investing in capital goods.

(I do not believe in selling at a low price and straining profitability. Selling at a low price can be a strategy to capture the attention of prospects. However, this approach cannot be sustained in the long run, as it erodes the profit margin and challenges the business's sustainability. One should focus on customer benefits, unique selling points, brand image, excellent service, and support. Discounts should be offered strategically to make the price competitive rather than selling at low prices. While preparing the proposal, I kept the price high enough to capitalise on cognitive bias).

Purchase Manager (Gopal): You understood me right. Budget is a constraint.

Salesperson (Unni): The division Managers approved this product, which means they are convinced of its quality and distinguishing features.

Purchase Manager (Gopal): I agree with you. They approved the product, but I can only buy it within my budget.

Salesperson (Unni): I can understand your position. Although the initial investment is slightly over budget, it ultimately benefits you in the long run. I can justify my price:

a. These desks are ergonomically designed to cater to your employees' requirements and aesthetics.

b. Our desks are warranted for 10 years, whereas our competitors' are warranted for 5 years. Our desks are warranted for an additional 5 years, saving future costs.

c. Our desks use less power, as per the test certificates. This will result in considerable long-term savings, reducing operating costs.

Purchase Manager (Gopal): I agree with your points, but they do not solve my budget problems.

Salesperson (Unni): We offer a more affordable desk option with a 5-year limited warranty. Would you like to consider it? (Decoy Effect.)

Purchase Manager (Gopal): Our managers have approved this model. Let us stick to this model.

Salesperson (Unni): This is a premium product. We assure you of the value for the price you pay. Since this is a premium product, we have a limited stock of these desks (Scarcity Effect). Many corporate companies have bought these desks, appreciating their features and benefits (Social Proof). If you opt for the less expensive model to save on costs, you will compromise on quality, lose the additional warranty and power-saving features, and incur higher long-term running costs (Loss Aversion). This purchase is an investment with a term of ten years or longer. We are here to support you 24/7. The employees will experience no work-related issues and will improve overall efficiency (Framing Effect).

Purchase Manager (Gopal): I am convinced about this. Let us solve my budget constraints.

Salesperson (Unni): I understand your view. Let us find a solution that benefits both of us. If you place a bulk order within a week for all the divisions in one Purchase Order, I can offer you the following benefits: (Reciprocity Principle).

a. To support your business and allow you to benefit from our desk, we can offer you a 5% additional discount on the total value of the bulk order. Please note that delivery and installation are provided at no additional cost (Reciprocity Principle).

b. Flexible payment options like 25% advance payment along with the order, 25% during delivery and installation, 25% after one month, and 25% after two months of installation. Thus, you get a staggered payment facility. (Anchoring Effect)

Purchase Manager (Gopal): This proposal seems OK to me. I appreciate your efforts to address my budget constraints. The additional discount and staggered payment will be acceptable to my management. Please provide me with the final proposal that includes all the above clauses, along with a written 10-year warranty statement for our records. I will forward it to the management for final approval and prepare the Purchase Order.

Salesperson (Unni): That is a good move. Our company policy is to help customers get value for their investments. I will make a revised proposal and email it within 3 hours. I will contact you tomorrow to receive the Purchase Order for desks for all divisions. Thank you for choosing us. I am confident that you will love our product.

The next day, I received the Purchase Order for the requirements for all divisions.

This deal was a feather in my cap. I could break our competitor's monopoly. The Integrated Adult ego state supports the Cognitive Selling sales approach and reframes the customer's mindset.

By integrating the Adult ego state with the Cognitive Selling approach, I could guide and support the customer in making a final decision. Indeed, the customer nodded.

11.2 The Contextual Connection:

When salespersons adopt the Integrated Adult ego state, they behave from a balanced, logical, and emotionally mature position. They focus on information and assumptions to analyse the situations unbiased and respond appropriately. In the previous example, the customer was adamant about the budget, and the salesperson, without losing his patience, found a solution to it. Similarly, salespersons often face angry customers. When a customer becomes enraged, it indicates that they are frustrated and something has gone wrong. Their needs may not be met in the expected way, or they may be severely treated. The customer may be in the Child ego state if they become emotional or the Critical Parent ego state if they become judgemental and react authoritatively. This becomes a challenge. The salesperson in the Integrated Adult ego state can help the angry customer cool down and retain the customer's trust and loyalty. I have faced situations where the customer became angry. I could overcome this situation by remaining calm and listening attentively to understand the reasons behind the anger. Be empathetic and apologise, regardless of whether it was our mistake or not. When the customer hears the salesperson say, "I apologise for what has happened" or "I can understand your situation," they become more accommodating. It is better to remain positive and give logical explanations to arrive at a solution quickly. Even when the problem is solved, contact them to get feedback on the solution provided. The Integrated Adult ego state transforms a negative experience into a positive one, making the customer loyal to us.

A psychologically developed salesperson transitions to the Integrated Adult ego state, which is crucial in effective selling. According to the UniK Psycho-Sales Model, salespersons operating from the Integrated Adult ego state exhibit the following qualities:

   a. In touch with the salesperson's potential.

   b. Committed and Responsible.

   c. Intelligence to solve problems.

   d. Ability to create and express affection.

The above factors help a salesperson adapt to the Cognitive Selling sales approach as explained below:

When salespersons know their strengths, abilities, and weaknesses, their communication becomes authentic, and relationships become genuine and respectful. They adapt the relevant ego state to understand the customer's perspectives and provide specific solutions. For example, a salesperson with excellent product knowledge can provide valuable insights to customers on the uses and benefits of products, thereby winning their trust.

The Adult ego state makes a salesperson committed and responsible. Customers feel comfortable dealing with salespersons who keep their promises and take ownership of their actions. If customers face problems with the products, salespersons work diligently to resolve them. This will strengthen their relationships, and customers will return for future requirements.

The Integrated Adult ego state prepares salespersons to combine rational analysis, creative thinking, ethical behaviour, and enthusiasm to solve problems. The ability to solve problems is crucial in Cognitive Selling, as tailored solutions can be offered to address customers' specific issues. This makes a salesperson reliable.

When the salesperson operates from the Integrated Adult ego state, they can connect emotionally to customers. This ego state facilitates active listening, logical thinking, rational discussions, customised solutions, and transparency, all of which are crucial for Cognitive Selling.

The above factors support the principles of Cognitive Selling, such as understanding customers' needs, analysing customer data to know customer behaviour, problem-solving, building long-term relationships, and Emotional Intelligence. All of these are instrumental in achieving higher customer satisfaction and loyalty.

The above explanations conclude that the Integrated Adult supports Cognitive Selling. The support is mainly because this ego state equips the salespersons to be methodical, understand the customer, present solutions, and respond logically, remaining calm and composed. The connection between the Integrated Adult ego state and Cognitive Selling is contextual, as their effectiveness depends upon the context in which they are applied. In the sales scenario, the salesperson must understand the customer's background and the circumstances under which the transaction occurs. This will help them to frame a solution that matches customers' preferences. This is conducive to selling successfully.

11.3 Building Blocks of Cognitive Selling:

Cognitive Selling involves understanding customer thought processes, behavioural patterns, preferences, and needs. This understanding enables us to develop sales strategies that enhance customer satisfaction.

The building blocks of Cognitive Selling are as follows:

A. Knowledge and understanding of the Customer. This is crucial in Cognitive Selling. A salesperson finds out what the customer wants before proposing a product or solution. When I meet a customer, I gather all relevant information, including their position, company details, and specific requirements. When he says he wants to buy chairs, I make it a point to know the reason behind the purchase. Is it for replacing the existing chairs or for a new project? What is the required quantity, budget, number of chairs, and design elements? Based on these, I arrive at the right chair to meet their requirements. Thus, understanding exactly what the customer needs from the salesperson helps fulfil their specific requirements and build trust.

B. Cognitive Scripts and Cognitive Bias: Cognitive scripts detail the steps and interactions to follow in the sales process. These scripts are developed through experience, thus making the selling process easier and more manageable. However, care should be taken not to make it a stereotype. A cognitive script for selling office chairs is given below:

1. Make a good first impression: Welcome or greet the customer pleasantly to make them feel comfortable and at home. Self-introduction to break the ice.

2. Know the customer before selling: Gather detailed information about their requirements, including the type of chair they need, its specifications, preferences, budgetary constraints, and other relevant details.

3. Suggestions: Provide suggestions for various chair models, detailing their features, benefits, prices, design factors, and other relevant information.

4. Use of Cognitive biases to influence purchase decisions. Depending on the situation, a salesperson can utilise cognitive biases to influence a customer's purchasing decision. The cognitive biases commonly used are as follows:

   a. Anchoring Bias: quoting a high price initially and later offering a discount to make the final price attractive compared with the initial price (anchor).

b. Scarcity Effect: Inform the customer that the chairs are available in limited stock to encourage quick action.

c. Social Proof: Utilise testimonials from satisfied customers to persuade potential buyers.

d. Authority bias: Certifications from authorities, experts, or celebrities lead to the perception of chairs as reliable and worthy of purchase.

e. Loss aversion: People tend to avoid loss rather than gains. Losing the health benefits or comfort of sitting by not purchasing chairs will be more compelling. These biases should be used strategically, depending on the customer's responses.

5. Clarify any doubts or concerns to prevent conflicts or complaints later on.

6. Provide an opportunity to try the chair to feel the sitting comfort.

7. Closing the sale confidently at mutually agreeable terms. Ask convincingly for the order, e.g., "Can you place the order now?" or "Can I process the order now?"

8. Thank the customer and express willingness to support them after the sale.

The above script explains the structure of a cognitive script. It is only a guideline for selling any product. The script can be modified to suit the customer and the product under consideration. I used the above script to sell guidelines for any product. Ultimately, the customer should receive all the necessary information about the product and its commercial terms, enabling them to make a confident purchase.

C. Vicarious Learning Approach: The importance of learning for both professional and personal growth is well established. Learning is continuous, and we learn even without conscious awareness. Vicarious learning enables a salesperson to acquire specific skills and sales techniques by observing colleagues or successful salespersons. When I joined the organisation as a salesperson, I learned vicariously by observing my senior salespersons and attending sales training programmes. The methods adopted by the champion salespersons to overcome the setbacks were a powerful lesson for me to handle similar situations in sales. Joining Toastmasters Club, studying counselling, and Transactional Analysis supported me in vicarious learning. This type of learning helps salespeople sharpen their skills and stay updated.

D. Data-Driven: Data becomes an integral part of Cognitive Selling as it helps in decision-making and formulating strategies for taking corrective actions. Some office furniture companies collect data from various sources, such as news media, directories, websites, and social media. They analyse the data to identify the target segment for selling, such as the financial sector. Such segments have similar operations, and their requirements are identical. A personalised approach can be adopted for each segment, tailoring products and messages to meet individual needs.

Data-driven methods enable organisations to forecast consumer behaviour and identify opportunities based on evolving market scenarios. Salespersons can identify and focus their energy on potential customers during interactions.

Data-driven approaches enable the monitoring of sales performance and the taking of corrective actions to refine strategies. This leads to continuous sales improvement by adapting to changing market conditions.

Cognitive Selling combines data-driven insights with psychological principles to foster stronger customer relationships and drive revenue growth.

E. Emotional Intelligence: The importance of Emotional Intelligence in salespersons has been recognised by organisations. Nowadays, when selecting sales personnel, organisations prioritise both the Intelligence Quotient (IQ) and the Emotional Quotient (EQ). Psychologically, emotional intelligence enables a salesperson to manage their own emotions and those of their customers. It is important in sales to maintain complementary transactions during sales meetings. The salespersons become empathetic, resilient, and intrinsically motivated. These qualities are essential for fostering teamwork, collaboration, and building strong relationships with customers. Thus, emotional intelligence gives inner strength to salespersons and contributes to their long-term success.

We have discussed the various stages of the UniK Psycho-Sales Model. The stages covered are:

1. Preparation before meeting a customer.

2. Interaction between the ego states of the salesperson.

3. Development of Integrated Adult Ego State.

4. The outcome of the Integrated Adult ego state supporting Cognitive Selling.

5. The building blocks of Cognitive Selling.

Now, it is time to discuss the outcome of the UniK Psycho-Sales Model.

Curious About the Next Insight... Dive In...

Chapter 12

UniK Outcomes

When we walk through the UniK Psycho-Sales Model, the salespersons focus on achieving exceptional results through their efforts, and customers feel valued, leading to repeat purchases. The UniK outcomes are enumerated below:

1. Focus on Personalisation: With the help of this model, salespeople can provide solutions that match customers' specific needs and requirements. We say, "We provide what you need." If a customer suffers from back pain due to poor sitting posture, I recommend an ergonomic chair with comprehensive features to address this issue. When the customer wants to avoid sitting for a long time while working, I propose a height-adjustable desk that allows him to work from both sitting and standing positions. When a salesperson offers personalised solutions, the sales process becomes more impactful.

2. Rapport Building: The customer should like the salesperson for continued sales. This model facilitates the development of rapport with customers. This is achieved by building trust, maintaining transparent communication, actively listening, and showing genuine interest in them. If time permits, I engage in pastime conversations with customers about their hobbies, interests in sports, or other common areas

of interest. If I know the customer is a Toastmaster, I discuss Toastmasters Club activities with them. If the customer is inquisitive about counselling, I discuss counselling-related matters. Sometimes, I discuss children's development with parents who are customers. Discussing non-work-related subjects has helped me develop rapport with customers. However, this has to be exercised with caution.

3. Understanding Needs and Presenting Solutions: This model enables salespersons to comprehend customers' needs and challenges. The procedures detailed in this model equip the salesperson to adopt complementary transactions from an Adult ego state and focus on information, not assumptions. The problem-solving abilities of the Adult ego state provide the right solutions tailored to the customer.

4. Efficient Response: 'Time is more valuable than money.' A prompt and meaningful response from a salesperson will captivate the customers' attention. The response becomes efficient when the salesman successfully helps the customer overcome cognitive biases, clarifies doubts, and makes informed decisions.

5. Closing Sales Amicably: This is a crucial aspect of sales. The procedures in this model clarify customers' doubts and agree on commercial terms. The Integrated Adult ego state and Cognitive Selling help the salesperson close sales by making informed decisions, communicating effectively, and overcoming objections.

6. Repurchase: This is very important for an organisation. As per the model, the Integrated Adult ego builds trust to instil confidence in the customer. Cognitive Selling enables us to understand customers' thought processes

and focuses on maintaining continuous engagement through follow-ups, social media, and other channels. The Integrated Adult ego state supports the Cognitive Selling sales approach, which aims to deliver customer satisfaction and foster long-term relationships, ultimately leading to repeat business. I have observed that repeat purchases are pretty standard in sales. I have been serving the same customers for over three decades. Customers come to me when they require furniture for new employees or when they undertake expansion projects. If the customer is progressive in business, it is advantageous to the salesperson.

The UniK Psycho-Sales Model empowers salespersons to succeed by leveraging their Integrated Adult ego state in Cognitive Selling. Salespeople enjoy selling, and customers enjoy satisfaction. They repeat purchases from the same salesperson, furthering their long-term relationships.

"Every salesperson can enhance productivity by strategically harnessing their Integrated Adult ego state in Cognitive selling."

The Journey Continues... Keep Discovering...

Bibliography

3 Ways to be More Adaptable - Self-Care Café. https://www.selfcarecafe.nl/self-care-wisdom/3-ways-to-be-more-adaptable

4 ways to tackle optimism bias. (2023, September 14). https://www.apm.org.uk/blog/4-ways-to-tackle-optimism-bias/

7 Professional Development Activities For Work - Jenn Drummond. https://jenndrummond.com/blog/7-professional-development-activities-for-work/

7 Tips for Effective Communication Skills. https://www.invajy.com/7-tips-for-effective-communication-skills/

9 cognitive skill examples and how to improve them. (n.d.). https://www.betterup.com/blog/cognitive-skills-examples

Academy, E., & Academy, E. (2023b, December 26). What Are the Ethical Considerations in Research Design? *Enago Academy*. https://www.enago.com/academy/what-are-the-ethical-considerations-in-research-design/

Admin. (2017, June 2). *Know Transactional Analysis to Improve Your Communication*. Wisdom Springs Training Solutions. https://wisdomspringstraining.com/know-transactional-analysis-to-improve-your-communication/blog/

Admin. (2024, November 30). *7 Ways to cope and avoid the Dunning-Kruger Effect*. Mind Help. https://mind.help/topic/cope-and-avoid/

Administrator, P. (2023, August 28). *The Formation of Life Scripts: Understanding the Influences That Shape Our Life Path*. Psylancer. https://psylancer.com/psychology-topics/the-formation-of-life-scripts-understanding-the-influences-that-shape-our-life-path/

Advice to the NYS Blue Ribbon Commission on Graduation Measures | Ed In The Apple. https://mets2006.wordpress.com/2023/01/06/advice-to-the-nys-blue-ribbon-commission-on-graduation-measures/

Aghayeva, K., & Ślusarczyk, B. (2019). Analytic Hierarchy of Motivating and Demotivating Factors Affecting Labor Productivity in the Construction Industry: The Case of Azerbaijan. Sustainability, 11(21), 5975.

Ali, S. R., & Menke, K. A. (2014, June). Rural Latino Youth Career Development: An Application of Social Cognitive Career Theory. *The Career Development Quarterly*, *62*(2), 175–186. https://doi.org/10.1002/j.2161-0045.2014.00078.x

Analyzing the self with transactional analysis - part 1 -. https://parimukti.com/transactional-analysis-as-a-way-of-analysing-the-self-part-1/

Anchoring | Brainkit. https://www.braink.it/principles/anchoring

Anderson, J. R. (2000b). *Learning and Memory: An Integrated Approach*.

Armstrong, R. (2025, January 10). Selling Smarter: Boosting sales with data insights and psychology. *Pillar Optimization Partners*. https://pop4success.com/blog/selling-smarter-boosting-sales-with-data-insights-and-psychology?form=MG0AV3

Arootah, & Arootah. (2023, October 6). *5 Types of Listening: How to Be a Better Communicator | Arootah*. Arootah | Arootah Empowers You With Technology, Coaching and Advisory. https://arootah.com/blog/professional-development/communication-influence/5-types-of-listening/

Artificial Intelligence in Business - A-Z Guide - Tech Pilot. https://techpilot.ai/artificial-intelligence-in-business-your-guide/

Ashley. (2023, January 28). *What is the Framing Effect (and 5 Ways to Avoid it!)*. Tracking Happiness. https://www.trackinghappiness.com/framing-effect/

Author, G., & Author, G. (2024, January 25). *6 Cognitive biases you can exploit to boost sales*. WordStream. https://www.wordstream.com/blog/ws/2018/12/06/cognitive-biases

Awesome. (2024, June 17). *Sales Closing Techniques: 8 Proven Strategies to Seal Deals*. Breakthrough3X: 3x Your Profits & Impact (NOT Your Stress). https://breakthrough3x.com/resources/sales-closing-techniques/

Babel. (2022, June 22). The framing effect and how it influences the way you make decisions. *Exploring Your Mind*. https://exploringyourmind.com/the-framing-effect/

Balto. (2022, August 19). *How To Identify and Overcome Unconscious Bias in Customer Service*. Balto. https://www.balto.ai/blog/how-to-identify-and-overcome-unconscious-bias-in-customer-service/

Bergland, C. (2023, June 30). *What Is Self-Serving Bias in Psychology?* Verywell Health. https://www.verywellhealth.com/self-serving-bias-7374682

Bermont, T. (2004a). *Cognitive selling: Proven Fundamentals & Techniques of the World's Most Effective Salespeople*. 10 Step Corporation.

Berne, E. (1964, January 1). *Games People Play*. New York: Grove Press.

Berne, E. (2010). *What do you say after you say hello: Gain control of your conversations and relationships*. Random House.

Berne, E. (2015, July 19). *Transactional Analysis in Psychotherapy*. Martino Fine Books.

Berne, E. (1961). Transactional analysis in psychotherapy. Grove Press, Inc., New York

Berne, E. (2016). *Games People Play: The Psychology of Human Relationships*. http://ci.nii.ac.jp/ncid/BA14284704

BetterUp. (2023, September 27). *Self-serving bias: What it is and how to stop it*. BetterUp. https://www.betterup.com/blog/self-serving-bias

Bizarreness Effect definition | Psychology Glossary | AlleyDog.com. (n.d.). https://www.alleydog.com/glossary/definition.php?term=Bizarreness+Effect

Blaess, N. (2024, July 27). 10 Cognitive biases brands can leverage to boost sales. *Nine Blaess*. https://www.nineblaess.de/blog/cognitive-biases-brands-can-leverage/#:~:text=Brands%20can%20harness%20our%20tendency,stock%20of%20a%20popular%20item.

Blum, K. (2020, October 8). Future of Sales 2025: Data-Driven B2B Selling to Drive Digital Commerce. *Gartner*. https://www.gartner.com/smarterwithgartner/future-of-sales-2025-data-driven-b2b-selling?form=MG0AV3

Botha, E. (2013, November 15). *Transactional Analysis resources and information*. Pinterest. https://www.pinterest.com.au/pin/557601997607222476/

Bridge Research Consulting | Interpretivism Research Philosophy: Unveiling Its Power and Potential. (n.d.). https://bridgeresearchconsulting.com/blog/post/interpretivism-research-philosophy-unveiling-its-power-and-potential

Brontén, G. (2019, February 21). *Cognitive bias: What it is, how it impacts sales.* Membrain. https://www.membrain.com/blog/cognitive-bias-what-it-is-how-it-impacts-sales

Brontén, G. (2021, April 27). *What Is Anchoring Bias and What Do Salespeople Need to Know about It?* Membrain. https://www.membrain.com/blog/what-is-anchoring-bias-and-what-do-salespeople-need-to-know-about-it

Brudner, E. (2022, February 2). *12 Essential Negotiation Skills For Salespeople.* https://blog.hubspot.com/sales/essential-negotiation-skills-for-salespeople

Bull's-eye transaction, Role of transactions in multiparty contracting. (n.d.). Ebrary. https://ebrary.net/158997/management/bull_s_transaction

Calisaan, B. (2023, December 1). *Self-Serving Bias: Definition, Impacts & Strategies to Mitigate It.* UpJourney. https://upjourney.com/self-serving-bias

Calm Editorial Team. (2024, July 16). *Abstract reasoning: impacts, examples, and how to use it — Calm Blog.* Calm Blog. https://blog.calm.com/blog/abstract-reasoning

Caputa, P. (2023, February 1). *Active Listening in Sales: The Ultimate Guide.* https://blog.hubspot.com/sales/active-listening-guide

Carnegie, D. (Ed.). (1998). *How to Win Friends and Influence People.*

Catalog. https://www.rssing.com/catalog.php?cen0=0&cen1=61&cen2=82&cen3=88

Caulfield, J. (2022, January 30). *What is optimism bias? Definition & examples*. Scribbr. https://www.scribbr.com/research-bias/optimism-bias/

Chand, S. (2014, February 24). *8 Mental Traits which are Required to Become a Successful Salesman*. Your Article Library. https://www.yourarticlelibrary.com/salesmanship/8-mental-traits-which-are-required-to-become-a-successful-salesman/1955

Chaplot, R. (2024, July 4). *Sales psychology: (6 proven techniques & tips)*. PSDCenter. https://www.psdcenter.com/sales-psychology/?form=MG0AV3

Chironna, M. J. (2023). Toward a Pentecostal theology of prophetic legitimacy. https://core.ac.uk/download/596423597.pdf

Clarkson, P., & Gilbert, M. (1988, January). Berne's Original Model of Ego States: Some Theoretical Considerations. *Transactional Analysis Journal, 18*(1), 20–29. https://doi.org/10.1177/036215378801800105

Claudia. (2019, December 14). *Ego States in Transactional Analysis. Learn TA now*. Basic Course Transactional Analysis. https://ta-course.com/ego-states/

Claudia. (2019b, December 14). *Transactional analysis explained - Quick and easy*. Basic Course Transactional Analysis. https://ta-course.com/transactional-analysis-explained/

CogniFit. (n.d.). Perception- Cognitive Ability CogniFit. https://www.cognifit.com/perception

Cognitive reasoning: How to find candidates with strong cognitive skills. (2022, March 17). TestGorilla. https://www.testgorilla.com/blog/cognitive-reasoning/

Communicating Your Value | Electric Impulse Communications. https://www.electricimpulse.com/resources/articles/communicating-your-value/

Confirmation bias. Retrieved September 10, 2024, from. (2024).

Confirmation Bias: How to Identify and Overcome It. https://www.verywellmind.com/what-is-a-confirmation-bias-2795024

Cooke, B. (2021, June 16). *Transactional Analysis And Ego States - Bob Cooke*. Bob Cooke. https://bobcooke.org/transactional-analysis-and-ego-states/

Corey, G. (2004, January 1). *Theory and Practice of Group Counseling*. Wadsworth Publishing Company.

Cornell, W. F., de Graaf, A., Newton, T., & Thunnissen, M. (2016). Into TA: A Comprehensive Textbook on Transactional Analysis. 1st Edition. London: Routledge

CRO-tool | The role of cognitive biases in Conversion Rate Optimization (CRO). https://cro-tool.com/blog/the-role-of-cognitive-biases-in-conversion-rate-optimization

D. O. (2014, December 1). *PPT - TA Diagrams PowerPoint Presentation, free download - ID:7085361*. SlideServe. https://www.slideserve.com/damian-ortega/ta-diagrams

Description of Transactional Analysis and Games by Dr. Eric Berne, MD. (2013, January 28). Eric Berne, M.D. https://ericberne.com/transactional-analysis/

Diluted transactions. (n.d.). PPT. https://www.slideshare.net/manumjoy/diluted-transactions

Dixon, M., & Adamson, B. (2013). *The Challenger sale: How to Take Control of the Customer Conversation*. Penguin UK.

Dmtorbi. (2023, September 14). *EGO STATES – Basics (Part 2)*. HEAL & GROW for ACoAs. https://acoarecovery.blog/2013/04/06/ego-states-basics-part-2/

Donchak, L., Klein, Y., & Stanley, J. (2023, June 22). *Future of B2B Sales: Building the right team and talent to drive growth in an uncertain environment*. McKinsey & Company. https://www.mckinsey.com/capabilities/growth-marketing-and-sales/our-insights/future-of-b2b-sales-building-the-right-team?form=MG0AV3

Don't be afraid of enemies who attack you. Be afraid of the friends wh... Quote by Dale Carnegie, How to Win Friends and Influence People - QuotesLyfe. https://www.quoteslyfe.com/quote/Don-t-be-afraid-of-enemies-who-2029

Dublino, J. (2024, November 5). *5 reasons why emotional intelligence matters in sales*. business.com. https://www.business.com/articles/why-eq-matters-in-sales/

Empowering Excellence with the Influence of Professional Doctorate in Sales and Marketing on Career Advancement. (n.d.). https://www.ebu.ac/blog/151-Empowering-Excellence-with-the-Influence-of-Professional-Doctorate-in-Sales-and-Marketing-on-Career-Advancement-blog.php?form=MG0AV3

Erskine, R. G. (1988). Ego structure, intrapsychic function, and defense mechanisms: A commentary on Eric Berne's original theoretical concepts. *Transactional Analysis Journal, 18*(1), 15-19.

Festinger, L. (1962). *A theory of cognitive dissonance*. Stanford University Press.

Finlay, L. (2015, December 14). *Relational Integrative Psychotherapy*. John Wiley & Sons.

Francis Bacon quote: It's not what we profess but what we practice that.... https://www.azquotes.com/quote/1310630

Frost, A. (2017b, July 28). 7 Cognitive Biases Salespeople Must Know to Close Deals [Cheat Sheet]. *Hubspot*. https://blog.hubspot.com/sales/cognitive-biases-salespeople-must-know-close-deals

Game analysis - Transactional Analysis. (n.d.). PPT. https://www.slideshare.net/manumjoy/game-analysis-33725636

GeeksforGeeks. (2023, April 6). *Qualities of a good salesman*. GeeksforGeeks. https://www.geeksforgeeks.org/qualities-of-a-good-salesman/

Global Work Glossary. (n.d.). *Multiplier*. https://www.usemultiplier.com/glossary/confirmation-bias?nowprocket=1

Gluckow, J. (2019, January 1). *Sales in a New York minute*. (n.d.). Sound Wisdom. https://www.soundwisdom.com/sales-in-a-new-york-minute

Goleman, D. (2012). *Emotional intelligence: Why It Can Matter More Than IQ*. Bantam.

Great salespeople are relationship builders who provide value... | Picture Quotes. https://www.picturequotes.com/great-salespeople-are-relationship-builders-who-provide-value-and-help-their-customers-win-quote-358064

Greatest-Quotations.com - Eric Berne - The destiny of every human being is decided by what goes on inside his skull when confronted.... https://greatest-quotations.com/search/eric_berne/36343/the-destiny-of-every-human-being-is-decided-by-what-goes-on.html

Harris, T. A. (1967). *I'm OK - You're OK*. http://books.google.ie/books?id=-XqpzwEACAAJ&dq=I%27m+OK-You%27re+OK+By+Thomas+A.+Harris+MD&hl=&cd=1&source=gbs_api

Hart, M. (2021b, October 3). Hyperbolic Discounting: How to Use This Psychological Bias to Sell More. *Hubspot*. https://blog.hubspot.com/sales/hyperbolic-discounting

Hartley, H. (2021, August 18). *Ulterior Transactions: The Hidden Depths of Our Relationships - The Rediscovery of Me*. The

Rediscovery of Me. https://rediscoveryofme.com/ulterior-transactions/

Helen, S. (2022, June 26). *Transactional Analysis resources and information.* Pinterest. https://www.pinterest.com.au/pin/141793088258946636/

Hindsight Bias ЪЛЬНЬ - by Julia Clavien - Mental Models Weekly. https://www.mmweekly.com/p/mental-models-issue-49-hindsight-21-10-16

Hoffman, B. (2024, August 1). The framing effect: what it is and how to overcome it. *Forbes.* https://www.forbes.com/sites/brycehoffman/2024/07/31/the-framing-effect-what-it-is-and-how-to-overcome-it/

How to Communicate Effectively With Health Care Professionals - Senior Health Care Hub. https://seniorhealthcarehub.com/how-to-communicate-effectively-with-health-care-professionals/

How to Sell Pressure Washing Business | Clean Marketing. https://cleanmarketing.net/proven-techniques-for-pressure-washing-lead-conversion/

Https://inass.org/wp-content/uploads/2022/05/2022083131-2.pdf. (2022). *International Journal of Intelligent Engineering and Systems, 15*(4). https://doi.org/10.22266/ijies2022.0831.31

HubSpot. (2024, September 29). *Cognitive biases salespeople must know to close deals.* https://blog.hubspot.com/sales/cognitive-biases-salespeople-must-know-close-deals

Hyperbolic discounting - The Decision Lab. (n.d.). The Decision Lab. https://thedecisionlab.com/biases/hyperbolic-discounting

Imagination - GoodTherapy.org Therapy Blog. (2015, August 10). GoodTherapy.org Therapy Blog. https://www.goodtherapy.org/blog/psychpedia/imagination

Impact of Brand Image on Consumer Behaviour of Luxury Goods in the Fashion Industry. https://www.tutorialspoint.com/impact-of-brand-image-on-consumer-behaviour-of-luxury-goods-in-the-fashion-industry

Importance of Reasoning: The Art of Thinking Well. (2023, September 16). Explore the Latest Blogs on Startups and Business Success. https://www.thinkwithniche.com/blogs/details/importance-of-reasoning-the-art-of-thinking-well

Internal transaction. (n.d.). PPT. https://www.slideshare.net/manumjoy/internal-transaction

Jacoby, D. (n.d.). *6 Cognitive Biases that Can Kill Your Sales Results.* https://www.salesreadinessgroup.com/blog/six-cognitive-biases-that-can-kill-your-sales-results

James, M., & Jongeward, D. (1981, January 1). *Born to Win: Transactional Analysis with Gestalt Experiments.*

Johns, M. (n.d.). *The Difference Between Skills & Abilities.* Thomas International. https://www.thomas.co/resources/type/hr-blog/difference-between-skills-abilities

Johnson, P. G. &. M. (2022, May 3). *The Psychology of Overcoming Egocentric Decision-Making — pop neuro.* Pop Neuro. https://www.popneuro.com/neuromarketing-blog/psychology-egocentricity-decision-making-marketing-consumer-behavior-choices

Jones, E. E. (1971). *The actor and the observer: Divergent Perceptions of the Causes of Behavior.*

Joseph, T. (2017, October 17). *Data-Driven Cognitive Selling - Aspire Systems.* Aspire Systems - Blog. https://blog.aspiresys.com/digital/big-data-analytics/data-driven-cognitive-selling/

Karve, A. (n.d.). *Transactional Analysis Theory - Types of Transactions.* https://tatheoryandpracticebyajitkarve.blogspot.com/2018/04/transactional-analysis-theory-types-of_7.html

Klein, A. (2018, October 4). *The Story of a Life - Therapy for People*. Therapy for People. https://therapyforpeople.com/the-story-of-a-life/

Knoesen, B. C. (2015). Exploring the communication skills of community pharmacists in the Nelson Mandela Metropole. https://core.ac.uk/download/327307981.pdf

Koopmans, L. & Leona Bishop. (2009). *The Integrating Adult is the most dynamic part of our personality.* https://functionalfluency.com/uploads/files/news/article-from-ego-states-to-functional-fluency-lieuwe-koopmans.pdf?form=MG0AV3

Lapworth, P., & Sills, C. (2011, May 12). *An Introduction to Transactional Analysis.* SAGE.

MacKinnon, B. (2010). *Ethics: Theory & Contemporary Issues - Concise Edition.* Cengage Learning.

Makela, R. (2021, June 16). *Is Empathy The Most Important Selling Skill?* Forbes. https://www.forbes.com/sites/forbesbusinessdevelopmentcouncil/2021/06/16/is-empathy-the-most-important-selling-skill/?sh=261f4b141505

Markowsky, G. (n.d). Physiology in information theory. *Britannica.* https://www.britannica.com/science/information-theory/Physiology

Marcos, L. R. A. J. (2014, August 7). *The (New) Skills You Need to Succeed in Sales.* Harvard Business Review. https://hbr.org/2012/08/the-changing-face-of-sales

Maria, G. (2021, July 8). *What Is Adaptive Selling? Moreover, How You Can Ace It.* GetApp. https://www.getapp.com/resources/what-is-adaptive-selling/

Martin, K. (2023, June 20). *Games People Play - Berne defined games.* Conjunction. https://www.conjunctio.co.uk/games-people-play/

Mastering the Art of Sales: Essential Training for Success. https://www.protouchpro.com/guest-posts/mastering-the-art-of-sales-essential-training-for-success/

Maxedon, S. S. (n.d.). *A Study of The Gallows Transaction*. The Keep. https://thekeep.eiu.edu/theses/3251/

McLeod, S., PhD. (2023). What Is Cognitive Dissonance Theory? *Simply Psychology.* https://www.simplypsychology.org/cognitive-dissonance.html?nowprocket=1

McPheat, S. (2024, December 19). *Understanding Cognitive Biases in Sales | MTD Sales.* MTD Sales Training. https://www.mtdsalestraining.com/mtdblog/cognitive-biases-in-sales.

Mefteh, K. C., & Akrout, F. (2024). Cognitive Neuroscience and Sales Performance: The Evolution of the Seller's Theory of Mind. *IntechOpen.* https://doi.org/10.5772/intechopen.114220

Mind Help. (n.d.). *How to cope with and avoid the Dunning-Kruger effect.* Retrieved September 28, 2024, from https://mind.help/topic/dunning-kruger-effect/cope-and-avoid/

Module 4: Implicit Bias & Microaggressions – Project READY: Reimagining Equity & Access for Diverse Youth. (n.d.). https://ready.web.unc.edu/section-1-foundations/module-4-implicit-bias-microaggressions/

Morton, R. (2025, March 4). *Psychological selling guide: How to better understand your leads.* Pipedrive. https://www.pipedrive.com/en/blog/psychological-selling-guide?form=MG0AV3

MSEd, K. C. (2023, April 18). *Cognition in Psychology.* Very well Mind. https://www.verywellmind.com/what-is-cognition-2794982

MSEd, K. C. (2023b, November 21). *Actor-Observer Bias in Social Psychology*. Verywell Mind. https://www.verywellmind. com/what-is-the-actor-observer-bias-2794813

MSEd, K. C. (2024, July 1). *How the Dunning-Kruger Effect Works*. Verywell Mind. https://www.verywellmind.com/an-overview-of-the-dunning-kruger-effect-4160740

MSEd, K. C. (2024, May 19). *What Is Confirmation Bias?* Verywell Mind. https://www.verywellmind.com/what-is-a-confirmation-bias-2795024

MSEd, K. C. (2024c, April 21). *What Does 'Cognitive' Mean in Psychology?* Verywell Mind. https://www.verywellmind. com/what-is-cognition-2794982

Multiplier. (n.d.). Confirmation bias. Retrieved September 10, 2024, from

Murray, H. (2023). Transactional Analysis Theory & Therapy: Eric Berne. *Simply Psychology*. https://www.simplypsychology. org/transactional-analysis-eric-berne.html

Navigating Moral Dilemmas in Leadership. https://aligntoday. com/blog/ethics-of-leadership

Neisser, U. (2014). *Cognitive Psychology: Classic Edition*. Psychology Press.

NeuroLaunch.com. (2024, October 18). *Goleman's Theory of Emotional Intelligence: A Comprehensive Exploration*. https://neurolaunch.com/goleman-theory-of-emotional-intelligence/?form=MG0AV3#google_vignette

Nickerson, C. (2023, October 10). *Prospect Theory in Psychology: Loss Aversion Bias*. Simply Psychology. https://www. simplypsychology.org/prospect-theory.html

Nickerson, C. (2023a, October 10). *Mere Exposure Effect in Psychology: Biases & Heuristics.* Simply Psychology. https://www.simplypsychology.org/mere-exposure-effect.html

Nikolopoulou, K. (2023, January 27). *What is optimism bias? Definition & examples.* Scribbr. Revised on October 5, 2023. https://www.scribbr.com/research-bias/optimism-bias/

Nikolopoulou, K. (2023, March 18). What Is the Egocentric Bias? | Definition & Examples. *scribbr.* https://www.scribbr.com/research-bias/egocentric-bias/

Niwlikar, B. (2024, March 8). *Transactional Analysis - Meaning, Ego states, Functions - Careershodh.* Careershodh. https://www.careershodh.com/transactional-analysis-meaning-ego-states-child-ego-parent-ego-adult-ego/

Optimism bias in sales - Bing. (n.d.). Bing. https://www.bing.com/search?q=optimism+bias+in+sales&toWww=1&redig=B4257CC23B00483DB17848E6CD8FCCC7

Optimism bias. (2024, August 21). Definition, Explanation, Examples, How to Avoid? https://www.wallstreetmojo.com/optimism-bias/

Pamela Barnett PhD - Memory consolidation. https://sites.google.com/site/prebarnett/neuroplasticity/memory-consolidation

Perera, A. (2023). Framing effect in psychology. *Simply Psychology.* https://www.simplypsychology.org/framing-effect.html

Perez, L. (n.d.). *The Impact of Buyer Behavior and Cognitive Biases on Sales Performance.* Showell. https://www.showell.com/resources/buyer-behavior-and-biases-impact-sales-performance

Pfeiffer Library: Research Methodologies: What are research methodologies? (n.d.). https://library.tiffin.edu/research methodologies/whatareresearchmethodologies

Pillai, A. V. (2021). Customer Happiness: The Role of Cognitive Dissonance and Customer Experience. In *Studies in Rhythm Engineering* (pp. 117–125). https://doi.org/10.1007/978-981-33-6374-8_7

Pipedrive. (2025, February 25). What is cognitive bias? 7 biases that can make or break your sales. *Pipedrive*. https://www.pipedrive.com/en/blog/cognitive-bias-sales

Popova, M. (2022, July 15). *Games People Play: The Revolutionary 1964 Model of Human Relationships That Changed How We (Mis)Understand Ourselves and Each Other*. The Marginalian. https://www.themarginalian.org/2022/07/12/eric-berne-games-people-play/

Qureshi, A. (2024b, July 10). *Transactional Analysis Therapy Explained: Your Path to Self-Understanding*. Therapy Helpers. https://therapyhelpers.com/therapy-types/what-is-transactional-analysis-therapy/

Rasta, A. (2025, January 12). *The future of B2B sales: Key trends to watch in 2025*. Sales & Marketing Management. https://salesandmarketing.com/the-future-of-b2b-sales-key-trends-to-watch-in-2025/?form=MG0AV3

Recker, H. (2023, March 13). *What Is Data Aggregation? (Examples + Tools)*. Coefficient. https://coefficient.io/data-aggregation

Ricee, S., Ricee, S., & Ricee, S. (2021, October 3). *Actor Observer Bias – How to avoid and improve your workpace? [2024 DEI Resources] | Diversity for Social Impact*. Diversity for Social ImpactTM. https://diversity.social/actor-observer-bias/

Roese, N. J., & Vohs, K. D. (2012). Hindsight bias. *Perspectives on Psychological Science, 7*(5), 411-426. https://doi.org/10.1177/1745691612454303

Roguska, Z. (2023, March 5). *The Anchoring Effect In Marketing: A Comprehensive Guide*. Peep Strategy. https://peepstrategy.com/anchoring-effect-marketing/

Roguska, Z. (2023, November 29). Leveraging the framing effect in marketing to increase sales. *Peep Strategy*. https://peepstrategy.com/framing-effect-in-marketing/

Rudzinska-Wojciechowska, J. (2017). If you want to save, focus on the forest rather than on trees. The effects of shifts in levels of construal on saving decisions. PLoS One, 12(5), e0178283.

Rules of communication. (n.d.). PPT. https://www.slideshare.net/manumjoy/rules-of-communication

Sales Funnel meaning in Hindi » TheHindiMeaning.in. https://thehindimeaning.in/sales-funnel-meaning-in-hindi/

Sales Skills Definition – Online sales training courses. (n.d.). https://thedigitalsalesinstitute.com/sales-skills-definition/

Sc-Admin. (2024, July 16). *Transactional Analysis: Understanding TA & Its Benefits*. SeraphCorp Institute. https://www.seraphcorp.net/understanding-transactional-analysis/#:~:text=The%20Benefits%20of%20Transactional%20Analysis&text=TA%20serves%20as%20a%20helpful,behavioural%20improvements%20and%20better%20communication.

Scribbr. (2022, May 9). *How can I minimize observer bias in my research?* https://www.scribbr.co.uk/faqs/how-can-i-minimise-observer-bias-in-my-research/

Scribbr. (n.d.). *The actor-observer bias*. Scribbr. Retrieved September 24, 2024, from https://www.scribbr.co.uk/bias-in-research/the-actor-observer-bias/

Shad, R., & Olukemi, A. (2024). *The Impact of Cognitive Biases on Consumer Decision-Making*. EasyChair Preprint 14017. Retrieved from EasyChair1.

Showcase, J. F. (2024, November 5). *The Future of B2B Sales: A Peek into 2025 and Beyond*. The Showcase Workshop Blog. https://blog.showcaseworkshop.com/the-future-of-b2b-sales-a-peek-into-2025-and-beyond/?form=MG0AV3

Singh, H. (2022, February 4). *Transactional Analysis*. Harappa. https://harappa.education/harappa-diaries/transactional-analysis/

Social Psychology. (n.d.). Google Books. https://books.google.com.bh/books?id=WXGUxpv9aSwC&lpg=PP1&pg=PR4&redir_esc=y#v=onepage&q&f=false

Sreekumar, D., & Sreekumar, D. (2023, August 31). *What is the Research Methodology? Definition, Types, and Examples*. Paperpal Blog. https://www.paperpal.com/blog/academic-writing-guides/what-is-research-methodology/

Stanley, C. (2012). *Emotional intelligence for sales success: Connect with Customers and Get Results*. AMACOM.

Stewart, I. (1996, April 19). *Developing Transactional Analysis Counselling*. SAGE.

Stewart, I. (2013, November 6). *Transactional Analysis Counselling in Action*. SAGE Publications Limited.

Stewart, I., & Joines, V. (1987). TA today: A new introduction to transactional analysis. Lifespace Publishing.

Surprising Quotes About The Dunning-Kruger Effect: A Closer Look At Self-Perception And Incompetence. https://quotesanity.com/surprising-quotes-about-the-dunning-kruger-effect-a-closer-look-at-self-perception-and-incompetence/

TA 101 Transactional Analysis Introductory Course Handbook. (2021, January 1).

Talk Fast - Dance Quicker - Archives. https://archive.philpin. com/2013/01/talk-fast-dance-quicker

Team, E. S. (2024, September 1). Understanding The Dunning-Kruger Effect Dynamics. *Adult Online Courses.* https:// esoftskills.com/the-dunning-kruger-effect/

The Egocentric Bias: Why It's Hard to See Things from a Different Perspective. (n.d.). https://effectiviology.com/egocentric-bias/

The Empathy Gap: Why People Fail to Understand Different Perspectives – Effectiviology. https://effectiviology.com/ empathy-gap/

The HubSpot Sales Blog | Meredith Hart (2). (2023, July 11). https://blog.hubspot.com/sales/author/meredith-hart/ page/2

The Individual Processes and Perception, Specialization of Perceptual Processes. https://civilserviceindia.com/ subject/Management/notes/the-individual-processes-perception.html

The Opposable Mind Guards Against Cognitive Biases. https:// www.chadly.net/The-Opposable-Mind-Guards-Against-Cognitive-Biases

"The Science Behind Agreement: Cognitive Biases and Persuasion Techniques" – Appnana Hack Codes. http:// appnana-hack-codes.com/the-science-behind-agreement-cognitive-biases-and-persuasion-techniques/

The value of getting personalization right—or wrong—is multiplying. (2021, November 12). McKinsey & Company.

https://www.mckinsey.com/capabilities/growth-marketing-and-sales/our-insights/the-value-of-getting-personalization-right-or-wrong-is-multiplying

Tomlinson, I. (2010, March 10). *Transactional Analysis Games*. https://manchesterpsychotherapy.co.uk/transactional-analysis-games/

Top 15 Customer Returns Reasons in 2025 & How to Avoid Them. https://chargebacks911.com/customers-returns/

Transactional Analysis - NATAA. (2009, April 23). NATAA. https://www.usataa.org/transactional-analysis/

Transactional analysis (TA). (n.d.). Welldoing. https://welldoing.org/types/transactional-analysis

Transactional Analysis (TA): Overview, Examples, and Effectiveness. (2023, March 9). The Human Condition. https://thehumancondition.com/transactional-analysis-ta-overview/

TRANSACTIONAL ANALYSIS 101 | Skills Universe. https://www.skills-universe.com/transactional-analysis-101

TRANSACTIONAL ANALYSIS by Gerald Corey - Google Search. (n.d.). https://www.google.com/search?q=TRANSACTIONAL+ANALYSIS+by+Gerald+Corey&oq=TRANSACTIONAL+ANALYSIS+by+Gerald+Corey&gs_lcrp=EgZjaHJvbWUqBggAEEUYOzIGCAAQRRg7MgYIARBFGDzSAQkxMjIxM2owajeoAgiwAgE&sourceid=chrome&ie=UTF-8

Transactional Analysis in Sales Communication. (2016, October 26). Small Business - Chron.com. https://smallbusiness.chron.com/transactional-analysis-sales-communication-12561.html

Transactional Analysis Theory, Model, Key Concepts, Types & Benefits. P. (2023, May 4). https://www.matrrix.in/blogs/transactional-analysis

Transactional Analysis. (n.d.). PPT. https://www.slideshare.net/jalasayanan/transactional-analysis-12757931

Transactional Analysis: what is it, and how will it help? - Dr Elaine Ryan. https://mytherapist.ie/therapy/transactional-analysis/

Transactions - Transactional Analysis | PPT. https://www.slideshare.net/manumjoy/transactions-33677298

Tsipursky, G. (2020). *The Blindspots Between Us*. New Harbinger Publications. http://books.google.ie/books?id=c--0DwAAQBAJ&printsec=frontcover&dq=The+blind+spot+by+Gleb+Tsipursky&hl=&cd=1&source=gbs_api

Tversky, A., & Kahneman, D. (1974). Judgment under Uncertainty: Heuristics and Biases. In *Science* (Issue 4157, pp. 1124–1131). https://www2.psych.ubc.ca/~schaller/Psyc590Readings/TverskyKahneman1974.pdf

Tversky, A., & Kahneman, D. (1981). The framing of decisions and the psychology of choice. *Science, 211*(4481), 453-458. https://doi.org/10.1126/science.7455683

Types of transactions. (2021, October 3). The Intact One. https://theintactone.com/2019/06/28/mpob-u3-topic-12-types-of-transactions/#goog_rewarded

Ulterior transaction. (n.d.). PPT. https://www.slideshare.net/manumjoy/ulterior-transaction

Ulterior transactions — what's beneath? - romasharma - Medium. (2023, March 17). *Medium*. https://medium.com/romasharma/ulterior-transactions-whats-beneath-18da543cf8fd

Understanding Cognitive Biases: How to Use Them to Your Advantage in…. https://www.upwardspiralgroup.com/blog/understanding-cognitive-biases-how-to-use-them-to-your-advantage-in-marketing-and-sales.

Understanding Transactions: Duplex Transactions. (n.d.). http://www.skillzone.de/persoenliches-wachstum/self-coaching/3268-understanding-transactions-duplex-transactions

UnniKrishnan, T. T. (2024). Identifying The Role of Integrated Adult Ego State in Cognitive Selling Approach: A Study on Office Furniture in The Kingdom of Bahrain [PD]. European International University.

VandenBos, G. R. (2013). *APA Dictionary of Clinical Psychology.* American Psychological Association (APA). http://books.google.ie/books?id=rKM6LgEACAAJ&dq=VandenBos,+G.+R.+(Ed.).+(2007).+APA+Dictio+nary+of+Psychology.+American+Psychological+Association.&hl=&cd=1&source=gbs_api

Vinney, C., PhD. (2024, September 28). *The Framing Effect: How Perception shapes Decision-Making.* Verywell Mind. https://www.verywellmind.com/the-framing-effect-in-psychology-8713689

Vuorenheimo, M. (2023). *Examining Cognitive Biases in Consumer Decision-Making at the Point of Purchase: Comprehensive Analysis through the Lens of the 4Ps Marketing Mix.* Bachelor's thesis, Aalto University. Available at Aalto University Repository.

Wall, D. (2025, February 5). The four levels of sales intelligence and how to apply them. *Fundz.* https://www.fundz.net/sales-intelligence-blog/the-four-levels-of-sales-intelligence-and-how-to-apply-them

Weak transactions. (n.d.). PPT. https://www.slideshare.net/manumjoy/weak-transactions

Weil, A. (2023, September 15). *Transactional Analysis at Work: Enhancing Leadership and Team Dynamics.*

https://www.wellness-institute.org/blog/transactional-analysis-at-work-enhancing-leadership-and-team-dynamics#:~:text=Conflict%20Resolution%3A%20TA%20offers%20tools,rational%20discussion%20and%20problem%2Dsolving.

Weil, A. (2023, September 15). *Understanding Transactional Analysis in Organizational Behavior.* https://www.wellness-institute.org/blog/understanding-transactional-analysis-in-organizational-behavior

Weinstein, N. D. (1980). Unrealistic optimism about future life events. *Journal of Personality and Social Psychology, 39*(5), 806-820. https://psycnet.apa.org/doi/10.1037/0022-3514.39.5.806

Welles, J. F. (2018, February 6). Cognitive Dissonance Revisited. *Neuroscience and Neurological Surgery, 2*(1), 01–01. https://doi.org/10.31579/2578-8868/025

Wendling, L. (2020, May 14). *Traditional selling: it's so dead - ColoradoBiz Magazine.* ColoradoBiz Magazine. https://www.cobizmag.com/traditional-selling-its-so-dead/

What are Ego States? (2021, September 14). Counselling Tutor. https://counsellingtutor.com/counselling-approaches/transactional-analysis/what-are-ego-states/

What is Brand Heart? (Brand Essence). https://www.blog.thebrandshopbw.com/what-is-brand-heart/

What is cognition? (n.d.-b). Haiku. https://www.dementiasplatform.uk/news-and-media/blog/what-is-cognition#:~:text=Cognition%20is%20a%20term%20for,to%20function%20as%20healthy%20adults

What is Cognitive Bias in Sales? (Explained With Examples) - Breakcold. https://www.breakcold.com/explain/cognitive-bias-in-sales

What is Cognitive Bias? Definition and Examples. https://dovetail.com/research/what-is-cognitive-bias/

What is Cognitive Dissonance in Sales? (Explained With Examples). (n.d.). https://www.breakcold.com/explain/cognitive-dissonance-in-sales

What is Cognitive Marketing and Why Should You Be Using It? (n.d.). https://www.insightsforprofessionals.com. https://www.insightsforprofessionals.com/marketing/customer-experience/what-is-cognitive-marketing

What is Progressive Discipline? Definition, Policy, Process - HiPeople. https://www.hipeople.io/glossary/progressive-discipline

What Is the Egocentric Bias? | Definition & Examples. (2023, March 18). Scribbr. https://www.scribbr.com/research-bias/egocentric-bias/#:~:text=Under%20the%20egocentric%20bias%2C%20we,other%20people's%20perspectives%20and%20feelings.

Wikipedia contributors. (2024, September 25). *Dunning–Kruger effect*. Wikipedia. https://en.wikipedia.org/wiki/Dunning%E2%80%93Kruger_effect

Wikipedia contributors. (2024, September 4). *Optimism bias*. Wikipedia. https://en.wikipedia.org/wiki/Optimism_bias

Yashinsky, D. (2023b, September 5). 15 Framing Effect Examples (2024). *Helpful Professor*. https://helpfulprofessor.com/framing-effect-examples/#:~:text=The%20framing%20effect%20is%20a%20cognitive%20bias%20where%20the%20way#:~:text=The%20framing%20effect%20is%20a%20cognitive%20bias%20where%20the%20way

www.ingramcontent.com/pod-product-compliance
Lightning Source LLC
Chambersburg PA
CBHW060527160726
47991CB00001B/212